THE LAW OF TOMORROW

BITCOIN, TOKENS, BLOCKCHAIN

AN INTRODUCTION FOR LAWYERS

PAUL STRICKLAND
NICK OBERHEIDEN
ALINA VENEZIANO

Disclaimer

This book is written for informational and educational purposes only. It does not create an attorney-client relationship with the reader. If you have questions about a specific legal problem or circumstance, you need to consult an attorney to discuss your legal question and the specific circumstances of your situation. Prior results do not guarantee similar outcomes. The reader is specifically admonished not to rely on any prediction or recommendation made by the authors in this book and that the opinions in this book do not necessarily represent the legal position of the authors when representing and advising clients. Nothing in this book is intended to constitute the provision of legal advice, tax or accounting advice, securities or investment advice, or compliance advice. All website disclaimers of www.federal-lawyer.com apply.

ISBN: 978-1-7368542-9-7 (Paperback)

ISBN: 979-8-9869142-0-6 (Hardcover)

ISBN: 979-8-9869142-1-3 (Ebook)

CONTENTS

TABLE OF CASES

TABLE OF STATUTES

FOREWORD

Imagine your law office without internet, without email, and without computers. Imagine running your business without a smartphone or a website.

The codependence of law and technology has changed how lawyers research, analyze, and communicate the law. Right now, your law practice is undergoing another visceral change; a transformation likely greater than the advent of computers in the 1980s.

Blockchain, the technology that enables cryptocurrency and digital tokens, will alter how attorneys apply and practice law in the days to come.

Your choice is simple. You can join the movement and imbibe its endless opportunities, or you can spurn and defy only to find that your business might turn into a quaint necropolis.

Our goal with this book is to aerate your practice.

All of us have heard of Bitcoin, cryptocurrency, blockchain, smart contracts, and artificial intelligence. Yet few have examined how these technologies might transform the practice of law. What are digital assets? Are digital assets securities? How do smart contracts work? Where do we draw the line between legitimate cryptocurrency and illegal money laundering? What is the government's view on cryptocurrencies?

We offer the atoms of this pullulating synthesis of law and technology for you to explore its opportunities and flourish your own practice—in the areas of litigation, government investigations, contract law, intellectual-property laws, or tax compliance.

The *Law of Tomorrow* arrives today.

ABOUT THE AUTHORS

Dr. Nick Oberheiden is the founder of Oberheiden P.C., a U.S. litigation and regulatory compliance law firm. Comprised of former Justice Department officials and retired FBI and U.S. Secret Service agents, Oberheiden P.C. is at the forefront of government investigations, litigation proceedings, and compliance advice in the areas of cryptocurrencies, blockchain technologies, and tokenization.

Alina Veneziano advises executives and corporate clients of Oberheiden P.C. in all aspects of securities law and blockchain technologies including, but not limited to, mining, DAO organizations, ICOs, NFTs, and SEC compliance. Currently awaiting her Ph.D. from London's King's College with an examination of early U.S. securities law, Alina holds degrees from Georgetown University Law Center (J.D.), NYU School of Law (LL.M.), and Western Governors University (MBA). She passed her CPA examination and is a licensed attorney in New York.

Paul Strickland represents businesses under audit or investigation with a special emphasis on civil and criminal IRS, FBI, SEC, FTC, and DOJ investigations. Paul has advised a plethora of clients on tokenization and blockchain projects, coin structuring, mining, and smart contracts. A former clerk to the Honorable Justice Richard W. Pollack of the Supreme Court of Hawai'i, Paul graduated from UC Irvine School of Law (J.D.) and practices with Oberheiden P.C. out of California.

Thank You

The authors thank **John Sellers** (former Senior Trial Attorney, U.S. Department of Justice), **Lynette S. Byrd** (former Assistant U.S. Attorney), **Gary A. Loeffert** (former FBI Special Agent in Charge, former Chief of Staff at FBI Headquarters), **Timothy E. Allen** (retired Special Agent, U.S. Secret Service), **Marie Kondzielski** (retired FBI Special Agent, CFE) and **Kevin Sheridan** (retired FBI Supervisory Special Agent) and many others for their immensely valuable contributions.

PART 1:

DIGITAL ASSETS

"[W]hat we view as money has changed over time. Cowrie shells once were such a medium but no longer are . . . our currency originally included gold coins and bullion, but, after 1934, gold could not be used as a medium of exchange . . . [P]erhaps one day employees will be paid in bitcoin or some other type of cryptocurrency. . . Nothing in the statute suggests the meaning of this provision should be trapped in a monetary time warp, forever limited to those forms of money commonly used in the 1930s."

Justice Stephen Breyer, U.S. Supreme Court[1]

1. *Wisconsin Central Ltd. v. United States*, 17–530 U.S. 585 (2018).

§ 1 A Brief History of Trading

Generations ago, humans relied on bartering for trading. We have since progressed from trading weapons for furs to exchanging digital goods.

Regardless of its form—goods for goods, goods for services, goods for government-issued currency, goods "on credit," goods for Bitcoins, or "tokenized" goods for cryptocurrency—all trading shares three common elements: money, value, and trust.

Money. "Money" is a multipurpose tool that represents a measure of payment. It provides a store of value and serves as a unit of account for goods and services.

Value. To trade, any good or service must have "value." What is considered of value can be both subjective and objective; it is dynamic. Societies today attach less value to animal skins and shells than those in the Middle Ages. A society's acceptance of money as currency—whether represented by a coin, commodity, service, or cryptocurrency—does not mean that it is "valuable." The parties to a transaction may not value money in the same manner. This elusive quantification of value is part of all trading and informs the concept of valuation.

> Meet Sam. Sam manufactures strong farm boots. On the other side of the transaction are Frank, a farmer, and Charles, a ballet dancer. As a farmer, Frank values the boots more than Charles. Thus, Sam may expect to charge and receive more from Frank than from Charles for the same asset.

This valuation concept holds true in a digital society. For example, while more than one individual may value the digital image of a cat, that valuation may increase for someone who loves, but is deathly allergic to, cats.

Trust. A party's willingness to enter a transaction with another party also requires trust that the goods or services exchanged are not faulty, that the money is genuine, and that individuals will perform their obligations in good faith.

Throughout history, the primary motivation for trade has remained the same: economic growth and sustainability. So how did bartering evolve to Bitcoin?[2]

1. OLD AGES

Bartering was first recorded in Egypt in 9000 B.C. and involved the trade of goods and services. For a bartering transaction to occur, each party had to have what the other party needed. The parties also had to ascribe a similar value to their exchange—quite a challenge without a standardized pricing system.[3]

That's why societies began to develop a commodity-based form of trading using precious metals like copper, gold, and silver. Tribes or groups with more resources engaged in trade with others who valued those surplus items.

Historians credit the Kingdom of Lydia (present-day Western Turkey) for the development of the first recorded coin currency in 600 B.C. At the time, raw metals were too burdensome for trading. The Kingdom began to mint gold and silver coins with stamped animal images and markings to establish denomination. These coins were durable, portable, and had intrinsic value as a raw material. Coin holders could repurpose the gold or silver to produce other valuable items such as jewelry.

As more societies adopted coin currencies, the new diversity of coins became cumbersome and resulted in an abundance of authenticity issues. Low-value coins flooded the markets, all under the auspices of a nascent counterfeit coin industry.[4] The need for centralization and standardization became evident.

2. CENTRAL BANKS

The Bank of Amsterdam opened in 1609 to boost the Netherlands' economy. Sweden created its central bank, the Riksbank, in 1668. The Bank of England, chartered in 1694 to finance England's war with France, helped internationalize financial institutions. The First Bank of

2. MIKE THORNTON, *History of Money: Financial History: From Barter to Bitcoin – An Overview of Our Economic History, Monetary System & Currency Crisis* (2016).
3. PETE ROGERS, *The History of Money: From Barter to Bitcoin*, https://www.welfordmanagement.com (2018).
4. *Id.*

the United States, chartered in 1791, held significant gold reserves and alleviated inflation that resulted from the colonial government's overuse of credit during the revolutionary war.

These banks authenticated currency, recorded transactions in accounting ledgers, stabilized value, and reduced processing times. As trust in these institutions grew, banks began to issue paper notes as a form of money and handled, processed, and stored "value" on behalf of individuals. Bank notes allowed customers to purchase goods or services in exchange for gold or silver coins.

Central banks institutionalized trust in trading and soon began to dominate the money supply. Subsequent technological innovations helped create a new form of trading: bank notes and "credit."

3. CREDIT CARDS AND MODERN BANKING TECHNOLOGIES

Despite the trading advantages of paper money, a significant disadvantage was that this currency lacked the owner's name. Anyone could steal someone's currency and have full access to its value. From the 1950s, consumers could obtain credit cards bearing their names. Trust increased, and the risk of theft, to which cash was susceptible, reduced. As a result, trade flourished.

Technology produced ATMs in the 1960s, online banking in the 1990s, and mobile digital payment systems in the early 2000s. It was not long before capital markets proliferated for initial trading and secondary trading purposes.

4. DIGITAL CURRENCY AND TOKENS

National central banking systems proliferated fiat currencies (for example, the U.S. dollar, the Euro, the Yen) and money issued by a government and not backed by a commodity (for example, gold).

Further technological advances paved the way for digital currencies.[5] In 2009, the first digital, or programmable, currency was born: Bitcoin. Bitcoin was unique because, distinct from fiat currency, governments did *not* issue or control the currency. Bitcoin was *decentralized*. Decentralization removes control over the currency from the central government authority and insulates it from traditional inflation or deflation.

In 2014, the Ethereum Blockchain, a decentralized, open source blockchain with smart contract functionality, introduced "tokens," which

5. HAN LINQI, *Trust, Currency, and Science: The Rise of the Fintech and Token Economy,* E3S Web Conf. Vol. 218, (2020).

it sold to investors in exchange for Bitcoin. Unlike digital currency such as Bitcoin, tokens represent digital assets that can be sold to investors or consumers based on their application, features, and function. What can be tokenized—and its value—remains inherently subjective.

SUMMARY

The forms, means, and sophistication of trading practices among individuals and societies have evolved with technology. The emergence of cryptocurrency and tokens underscores a dynamic and changing understanding of money, value, and trust. Societal non-acceptance, economic failure, and legislative restrictions (or even prohibitions) are likely to abound.

§ 2 Blockchain

"Blockchain" is the technology behind the creation of Bitcoin and other cryptocurrencies. A blockchain is a permanent record of all transactions within a certain ledger. Each "block" contains the details of several transactions, and each block references the prior block, creating a linked chain. Blockchains operate on peer-to-peer networks—groups of computers that are connected. Each computer, or node, in the network keeps track of all blocks, and therefore all transactions.[6] Every participant has their own copy of the full ledger, which makes it unfeasible to manipulate.

Each new transaction is recorded in a block. Once the computer nodes on the network verify the transaction, the block links with the chain of prior transactions and becomes part of the permanent ledger, independently verified by each individual node.[7] This interconnectedness makes the blockchain a shared and reliable public ledger.

How do blockchain-based cryptocurrencies work? It starts with a simple transaction.

> Anna buys an office chair from Harry and pays with Bitcoin. This first step sends a transaction request into the system. A block is created that contains the transaction's details, as well as the previous block's digital key, or "hash." The transaction block then transfers to the network nodes in the blockchain, which begin their validation of the transaction by performing complex mathematical equations to find the new block's hash. The first node to solve the problem shares the correct solution with the network, and once at least 51% of the nodes confirm the solution, the block adds to the blockchain and becomes a permanent record.[8]

---

6. NEIL TIWARI, *The Commodification of Cryptocurrency,* 117 Mich. L. Rev. 611, (2018).
7. ADEL BEN MNAOUER & LAMIA CHAARI FOURATI, *Enabling Blockchain Technology for Secure Networking and Communications*, (2021).
8. RAMAKRISHNAN RAMAN & BENSON EDWIN RAJ, *The World of NFTs (Non-Fungible Tokens): The Future of Blockchain and Asset Ownership, Ch. 5 in Enabling Blockchain Technology for Secure Networking and Communications,* at 89-108, (2021).

CEO and Executive Director of the Stellar Development Foundation, Denelle Dixon, provides this blockchain description:

> [B]lockchain allows value and money to flow just like email. So, it's very simple in terms of how it can get from one point to another. And it does so very, very quickly. The importance of that is it can cross borders much more simply than anything else that's out there today. So, the value of blockchain is the ability to send from the United States, for example, and send to another country without having to reconcile with all the different software and intermediaries that exist today. So, it eliminates intermediaries.[9]

Blockchain's decentralized nature allows users to participate in direct transactions with one another without third-party intermediaries such as banks, brokers, and governments overseeing its operations. Any member of the public can view the history of transactions on a blockchain.[10]

1. THE PILLARS OF BLOCKCHAIN TECHNOLOGY

Blockchain technology has eight pillars critical to its operation that ensure financial sustainability and security in online transactions.[11]

- ***Decentralization***: No single authority, entity, or government controls the blockchain. The Bitcoin Blockchain is a decentralized, permissionless network.
- ***Distributed Ledger***: The blockchain is shared across a network of users. Its distributed nature precludes data loss, as many users, or computer nodes, have a copy of the ledger.
- ***Validation Procedures***: Individuals and businesses can verify and validate data transferred to the blockchain.
- ***Finality***: No one can modify or cancel the information on the blockchain. It is final.

9. REV.COM, *Crypto CEOs Testify Before House Financial Services Hearing Transcript,* rev.com, (Dec. 8, 2021).
10. DEAN W. KORSAK & ERIK FUQUA, *Decrypting Bitcoin and Blockchain for Military Lawyers,* JAG REPORTER, (2021).
11. ADEL BEN MNAOUER & LAMIA CHAARI FOURATI, *Enabling Blockchain Technology for Secure Networking and Communications,* (2021); RAMAKRISHNAN RAMAN & BENSON EDWIN RAJ, *The World of NFTs (Non-Fungible Tokens): The Future of Blockchain and Asset Ownership, Ch. 5 in Enabling Blockchain Technology for Secure Networking and Communications,* pp. 89-108, (2021); JOHN TASKINSOY, *Bitcoin Could be the First Cryptocurrency to Reach a Market Capitalization of One Trillion Dollars,* (2020).

- ***Immutability***: No one can alter transaction data. If someone tries to alter transaction data on a block, the entire hash, and the hash of the prior block, will change. The other nodes will notice this attempted change and prevent it from happening.
- ***Consensus Algorithm***: Blocks are created using a consensus method such as proof-of-work or proof-of-stake. Once validators reach a consensus, the block transfers to the blockchain.
- ***Secure***: The blockchain is resistant to hacking, tampering, and cyberattacks.
- ***Transparency***: All users across the network can view and track transactions on the blockchain.

2. BLOCKCHAIN DISTINCTIONS

Public Blockchain vs. Private Blockchain. Public blockchains are networks anyone can join without participation restrictions. Private blockchains are platforms for a single company's internal system and are not publicly available.

Permissionless vs. Permissioned. Blockchains can be either permissionless or permissioned. Permissionless blockchains have no restrictions on who can access them or verify transactions. Permissioned blockchains are closed networks, partially decentralized, and distributed across known parties. Ripple and Facebook's Libra coin are examples of permissioned blockchains. Facebook announced that a permissioned payment system with the coin "Diem" will run on its blockchain network. Both Libra and Diem are not decentralized and will run first on permissioned blockchains. Facebook plans for Diem to give the world access to financial services by using blockchain technology

Private Key vs. Public Key. To send Bitcoin, you need to have (1) your public key, (2) your private key, and (3) the recipient's public address. The public key is a user's public address to which others can send bitcoins. The private key is like a password known only to the individual user and links to a user's public address.[12] The public keys of the transaction are viewable by anyone with internet access, but the names of the individuals linked to the public keys are not viewable. Bitcoin transactions are *pseudonymous*, not anonymous.

Proof-of-Work vs. Proof-of-Stake. Two mechanisms verify transactions: proof-of-work and proof-of-stake. Proof-of-work involves a community with equal access to a blockchain using their computer power to solve mathematical algorithms to verify transactions in exchange for

12. DEAN W. KORSAK & ERIK FUQUA, *Decrypting Bitcoin and Blockchain for Military Lawyers*, JAG REPORTER, (2021).

coin rewards. The less common proof-of-stake allows users to validate transactions in proportion to how much of the cryptocurrency they hold. Those who hold more coins have more verification power.

3. BLOCKCHAIN POSSIBILITIES

At a December 2021 hearing involving testimony of crypto CEOs, the Ranking Member of the House Financial Services Committee said the following:

> 2021 was the year of the cryptocurrency. More Americans than ever are taking notice of this transformational technology. [...] Technology and its adoption are moving fast. Entrepreneurs and innovators are building and deploying the next generation of the internet. [...] This technology is new and exciting. It promises a new direction for financial economies, services, and products.[13]

How has blockchain changed the way people do business? Think of start-ups. In the past, a start-up needed an angel investor willing to invest capital in their business plan—usually in exchange for an ownership interest. Once the company had capital, a business plan, and public interest, it launched an initial public offering, or "IPO." IPOs are costly, and the regulatory requirements are cumbersome—even if the company proceeds under a registration exemption. Blockchain rewrites this equation.

Entrepreneurs can now use blockchain technology to raise capital through peer-to-peer networks in online offerings. Initial coin offerings (ICOs) are replacing traditional IPOs to raise money with online coins without federal regulatory oversight and transaction fees. Online offerings through peer-to-peer networks democratize participation in capital formation.[14]

Tech giants now offer blockchain technology on their platforms. For instance, Amazon's Managed Blockchain feature allows users to create their own private blockchain networks, build their own applications, and invite other users with open-source frameworks Hyperledger Fabric (private and permissioned) and Ethereum (public and permissionless).[15] Twitter allows users with a mobile iOS device to accept tips in Bitcoin,

---

13. REV.COM, *Crypto CEOs Testify Before House Financial Services Hearing Transcript,* rev.com, (Dec. 8, 2021).
14. ALEX TAPSCOTT & DON TAPSCOTT, *How Blockchain Is Changing Finance,* HARVARD BUSINESS REVIEW, (2017).
15. AMAZON, *Amazon Managed Blockchain,* AWS.amazon.com, (last visited Apr. 22, 2022).

with Android functionality to come soon.[16] Twitter is also working on turning its payment company, Square, into a decentralized Bitcoin-exchange platform.[17]

With these tech giants promulgating blockchain technology, the value of cryptocurrencies rises. Crypto appreciation was further boosted on October 15, 2021, when the Securities and Exchange Commission (SEC) approved the first U.S. Bitcoin future exchange traded funds (ETFs). Bitcoin's price climbed over $60,000.[18]

Various U.S. states are also taking important steps in the crypto sphere. Wyoming has passed crypto-friendly laws, including a law permitting U.S. banks to hold both fiat currencies and cryptocurrencies. Wyoming Senator Cynthia Lummis has stated that she "would like to see cryptocurrency like Bitcoin become part of a diversified asset allocation that are used in retirement funds and other opportunities for people to save for the future."[19]

4. BLOCKCHAIN AND SMART CONTRACTS

A smart contract is a computer code that executes a set of embedded rules when a predetermined event occurs. Smart contracts exist on the blockchain. Thus, no one can alter them once they become part of the chain.

This inalterability differentiates smart contracts from traditional contracts. There is no "contract interpretation" or "contract modification," and there can be no breach in that sense.[20] Individuals program the "contract" to do something at a certain time—for example, releasing funds once a year on a specified date, transferring title to a buyer upon securing financing, or sending payment to a vendor once the buyer receives goods. The smart contract is an innovation because it bypasses contract negotiation and reduces the need for intermediaries.

---

16. LANDON MANNING, *Twitter to Integrate Bitcoin Tips for Users,* NASDAQ.com, (2021).
17. VISHNU V., *Twitter CEO Jack Dorsey Plans to Make Square a Platform for Decentralized Bitcoin Exchange,* Republicworld.com, (2021).
18. HASSAN MAISHERA, *U.S. SEC Finally Approves a Crypto ETF. But it is a Bitcoin Futures ETF,* FXEmpire.com, (2021).
19. CAMOMILE SHUMBA, *Wyoming's Crypto-Backing Senator Cynthia Lummis Bought the Bitcoin Dip and Loaded Up on $50,000-100,000: Filing*, Business Insider, (Oct. 8, 2021).
20. ALEX LIPTO &, STUART LEVI, *An Introduction to Smart Contracts and Their Potential and Inherent Limitations,* Harvard Law School Forum on Corporate Governance, (2018).

5. VARIOUS INDUSTRY SECTORS

Blockchain is set to transform many industry sectors and intermediary functions, including risk management, audit procedures, supply-chain management, banking, and tax, among others.[21]

The banking industry is an apt example. If an individual deposits a check on Friday afternoon, it may not clear until the next business week. With blockchain technology, the banking transaction completes instantly. To catch up with technology—and customers' expectations—Bank of America launched its cryptocurrency research division,[22] and JPMorgan Chase now provides all clients with access to Bitcoin and other cryptocurrency funds.[23] JPMorgan even created the "JPM Coin" on a permissioned shared ledger that allows some of its clients to transfer payments around the world.[24]

Blockchain technology can secure sensitive and confidential information such as medical records or attorney-client privileged communications. Just think about the advantages: imagine a world where political voting is safe because voter identities are identified, and double voting is impossible.

As Charles Cascarilla, CEO and co-founder of Paxos, explained, blockchain can be used to simplify everyday transactions and activities:

> Digital assets and blockchain technologies can create a more efficient, secure, and innovative financial system, and a more exclusive and equitable global economy. [...] The current system is expensive and slow. International and even domestic money transfers can take days. At any given time, there are trillions of dollars' worth of capital held up in transactions that have not yet settled. Digital assets are vastly more accessible. Anyone with a smartphone can download a wallet app to send and receive assets. No bank account is required. Transferring digital assets is instantaneous and convenient. They can be sent or received 24/7. There's no waiting around for wire transfers or money orders to arrive, or for banks and stock exchanges to open, and transfers are often very inexpensive, in some cases costing just a penny per transfer. Digital assets can also reduce bias in finance. At its heart, blockchain is just a math equation. It is agnostic to a user's race, gender, nationality, or income. And blockchain permanently and

---

21. ALEX TAPSCOTT & DON TAPSCOTT, *How Blockchain Is Changing Finance*, HARVARD BUSINESS REVIEW, (2017).
22. SAM MARTIN, *Bank of America is Bullish on Digital Assets; Believes Bitcoin is Only the Beginning*, Blockworks.co, (2021).
23. EMILY MASON, *Bitcoin About-Face: JPMorgan Opens Crypto Trading to All Clients*, Forbes.com, (2021).
24. JPMORGAN, *J.P. Morgan Creates Digital Coin for Payments*, (2021).

> publicly records transactions, reducing errors, fraud, and systemic risk. A blockchain-based financial architecture could settle trades on the same day, thus mitigating counterparty risk and eliminating the need for costly central clearinghouse.[25]

Consider the real-estate industry. Traditionally, buying a home requires that parties interact with banks, brokers, real estate agents, insurance, and title agencies—often on a face-to-face basis. Given the processing time needed to conclude a transaction, people have considered real estate to be an illiquid asset. Moreover, the real-estate industry has historically provided little transparency. Consider the 2008 housing market crash and how its attendant lack of transparency wreaked havoc on markets—especially for individual owners and tenants.

Blockchain technology changes the equation. Third-party intermediary individuals and services are eliminated with smart contracts. Once the transaction's predetermined conditions occur—for example, securing a mortgage and verifying title—the smart contract automatically executes its terms, including transferring title and recording deeds and mortgages.

The tokenization of real estate is more than a trend. Tokenization fractionalizes pieces of real estate into smaller tokenized pieces that issuers can offer to a broader pool of investors. Investors who could not purchase real estate in the past because of price barriers can now purchase an affordable piece, a tokenized share.[26] Owners selling property don't need to wait for buyers to purchase the entire property. They can generate capital through tokenized sales.

Blockchain technology also renders real-estate data immutable. Fraud and manipulation are almost impossible when dealing with information transferred and stored on the blockchain. The real estate industry will experience enhanced consumer confidence.

The advantages of blockchain technology to real estate transactions are broad. Property developers and architects can securely store their designs, engineering plans, and other construction documents on the blockchain. Real-estate agents and managers can throw away the piles of papers and store all their property details in one secure place, whether this includes price and property details or the lease itself. Tenants also stand to benefit, as they can make service or maintenance requests through the blockchain.

Under the leadership of Mayor Francis X. Suarez, Miami, Florida has established itself not just as one of the most innovative, most thrilling, and most sought-after places to live—but also a globally admired

25. REV.COM, *Crypto CEOs Testify Before House Financial Services Hearing Transcript*, rev.com, (Dec. 8, 2021).
26. STEVE STREETMAN, *Cryptocurrency and Real Estate*, (2021).

epicenter of commerce. Part of the success story are new technologies. Like few others, Mayor Suarez embraced—early on—the potential of arising technologies as seen in the transformation of Art Basel into one of the world's premier NFT exhibitions as well as the introduction of the MiamiCoin. The MiamiCoin is designed to fund resources to combat homelessness, food shortages, and to improve the overall life quality for Miami residents[27]. Mayor Suarez explained:

> Funds that will directly impact the lives of all our residents! It is generating $2000 every ten minutes and over $5 million in the last 30 days so it's on pace to raise about $60 million. [...] [I]t's not an involuntary tax and it's not philanthropy. [...] It's something that is completely different and could revolutionize the way governments are funded in the future. [...] It is theoretically possible that the city of Miami, through MiamiCoin, could generate enough taxes so that our residents don't have to pay one cent in taxes. That would be revolutionary.[28]

Like many start-up projects, the MiamiCoin has experienced setbacks and has faced some market-related obstacles. The seeds of pioneering innovation, however, continue to spread.

SUMMARY

Blockchain is transforming the way businesses conduct day-to-day transactions. Blockchain's features—immutability, security, and transparency—enable users to record transactions and events. Add in smart contracts, and the world is ready to build endless applications for varying purposes in a streamlined and efficient manner.

---

27. ALICIA WARREN, *Miami Mayor Defends Bitcoin After JPMorgan CEO Dimon Calls It 'Worthless,'* FoxBusiness (Oct. 12, 2021); TALIA KAPLAN, Miami-Specific Crypto Could 'Revolutionize the Way Governments are Funded:' Mayor Suarez, FoxBusiness (Sept. 20, 2021).
28. TALIA KAPLAN, *Miami-Specific Crypto Could 'Revolutionize the Way Governments are Funded:'* Mayor Suarez, FoxBusiness (Sept. 20, 2021).

§ 3 Bitcoin

In the 2008 white paper "Bitcoin: A Peer-to-Peer Electronic Cash System," an individual (or individuals) using the pseudonym Satoshi Nakamoto outlined a digital currency built upon peer-to-peer networks.[29] This digital currency, Bitcoin, launched in 2009, priced at around $0.0008 per Bitcoin. Today a single bitcoin is worth over $40,000.

Like currency, Bitcoin is transferable, portable, and scarce. But as a virtual currency, there are no physical coins—just a representation of value. Bitcoin offers lower transaction fees, pseudonymity, and transactional speed. Acceptance of Bitcoin is growing. This acceptance stems from its decentralization—it is free from central governmental control, with its value turning on the laws of supply and demand.

People have often compared Bitcoin to gold because both are precious, valuable, and mined. Yet Bitcoin offers several advantages over gold. If an individual were to find a cache of gold under their house, the discovery may affect the market supply of gold and inflate its price. Such inflation is a natural consequence of mining physical commodities where the production rate occurs at irregular schedules.

By contrast, the Bitcoin algorithm permits mining of only a certain number of coins at any time. Bitcoin's entry into the marketplace therefore occurs at regular intervals. Even if more people become Bitcoin miners, the number of Bitcoins remains static.

Wyoming Senator Cynthia Lummis summarized the benefit of decentralized Bitcoin vs. traditional fiat money:

> In the case of U.S. fiat currency, inflation is baked into the Federal Reserve's plan for the U.S. dollar. So, it's no wonder that our buying power is eroded...That will not be the case with Bitcoin. Bitcoin provides a more stable value to people who are either saving now

---

29. SATOSHI NAKAMOTO, *Bitcoin: A Peer-to-Peer Electronic Cash System,* (2008).

to live comfortably in the future but also people who are on fixed income or approaching fixed income now...[30]

People have engaged in Bitcoin transactions for many reasons, such as convenience, speed, pseudonymity, investment, governmental distrust or anxiety, and libertarianism. Despite some market corrections, digital currency remains in high demand and has arguably reached mainstream acceptance. For example, in 2019, a U.S. tax refund service named Refundo announced its partnership with Bitpay to allow U.S. taxpayers to receive their tax refunds in Bitcoin.[31]

1. MINING BITCOINS

Where do bitcoins come from?

Bitcoin's supply and circulation occurs through mining. Mining verifies transfers to the blockchain for a permanent record. Every time an individual makes a Bitcoin transaction, miners must validate the transaction by solving a complex mathematical problem to find the digital key to each block—the hash. The miner who solves the problem shares the solution with the other miners to validate the solution. This consensus validation mechanism is known as a "proof-of-work." A confirmed transaction, or "block," is added to the blockchain.

As an incentive, a miner receives a reward each time they produce a block, which is about every ten minutes. A single computer lacks the power to mine alone, so each crypto miner must be a member of a crypto mining pool to share computational resources. The first pool to solve the equation distributes the reward to pool members in proportion to their individual contribution.[32] In time, miners will mine less Bitcoin because the mathematical equation will have become too complex for most miners to solve and doing so will consume vast amounts of energy.[33]

Mining requires powerful computers, sophisticated computer software, and internet connection to run all day, every day. In Bitcoin's infancy, miners performed cryptocurrency mining on their central processing units (CPUs). CPUs, however, have limited processing

30. EMILY GRAFFEO, *An Incoming Senator Believes Bitcoin is a Better Store of Value than Paper Money and Plans to Teach Congress How to Use It to Reduce the National Debt,* businessinsider.in, (Dec. 15, 2020).

31. YOGITA KHATRI, *U.S. Income Taxpayers Can Now Get Refunds in Bitcoin,* coindesk.com, (2019).

32. ERIC D. CHASON, *How Bitcoin Functions as Property Law,* 49 Seton Hall L. Rev. 129, (2018); EUNY HONG, *How Does Bitcoin Mining Work?* investopedia.com, (2021).

33. DAVID MALONE & K.J. O'DWYER, *Bitcoin Mining and its Energy Footprint,* at 280-85, (2014).

speeds and consume vast amounts of energy. Today, miners rely on graphics processing units (GPUs), which are more powerful and effective than CPUs for mining operations. Other miners may use an application-specific integrated circuit (ASIC), which is a chip designed for a specific use (here, mining). As cryptocurrencies flourish and the number of miners increases, mining firms focus on ASICs.

2. BITCOIN AND BLOCKCHAIN PERMANENCE

For currency (fiat or crypto) to have value, a person cannot spend it more than once. Consider these scenarios:

- Scenario 1: Jane agrees to buy a hat from Joe for $5 cash, gives him the $5, and receives the hat. Jane cannot then go to Bill and spend that $5 again because she already gave it to Joe. There are no double-spending issues with a "cash for cash" transaction.
- Scenario 2: Jane buys a hat from Joe for $5 on credit. She promises to pay Joe in one week and records this amount in a ledger. Joe is satisfied and gives Jane the hat. Jane then scratches out this transaction in her ledger and buys a pair of shoes from Bill with the same $5. Jane records this transaction. Bill gets paid, and Joe doesn't. Jane's ledger manipulation has caused serious trust issues and led to third-party assistance (see Scenario 3).
- Scenario 3: Jane buys a hat from Joe for $5. Jane's bank records a deduction of $5 from Jane's account and an addition of $5 to Joe's account. Joe trusts that the third-party bank will accurately record, transfer, and process the $5, so he gives Jane the hat.

Like the bank in Scenario 3, the blockchain technology behind Bitcoin solves the double-spending problem. The record on the blockchain is immutable and ensures that individuals cannot spend Bitcoins more than once. For example:

- Scenario 4: Jane buys a hat from Joe for $5 and pays for it with Bitcoin. The Bitcoin transaction transfers to the blockchain, which stores a permanent record of the payment. Jane cannot go to Bill and try to spend the same $5. Thus, the result is the same as Scenario 3 above, except there is no third party or intermediary needed.

3. BITCOIN'S PRICE HISTORY

In 2010, Laszlo Hanyecz bought two pizzas from Papa John's and paid with 10,000 bitcoins—worth about $41 at the time. In 2021, the same 10,0000 bitcoins were worth over $630 million. Bitcoin enthusiasts have since declared May 22, 2010, as "Bitcoin Pizza Day."

Bitcoin's price history from 2009 to the present has been arbitrary and volatile. In January 2009, Satoshi Nakamoto mined the first block of bitcoins, which returned a reward of fifty bitcoins priced at $0 ($0.0008 per Bitcoin). By October, the price rose to $0.10 per Bitcoin, reaching about $0.39 by the end of the year. In 2011, Bitcoin's price climbed to one U.S. dollar per Bitcoin. A year later, Bitcoin grew from $2 to $13. The price of Bitcoin soared to above $200 by the start of 2013, peaking at over $1,000 and closing the year at about $750. Bitcoin closed at a little over $400 in 2015 and then climbed to over $19,800 in 2017.

Some attribute the rise in institutional investor interest. Others believe that a crypto whale (a person holding enough digital currency to affect its value) manipulated the market. Regardless of its cause, the price spike was short-lived. Bitcoin crashed to $3,900 in late 2018, leading to forecasts of the end of cryptocurrency. The exact opposite occurred.

Bitcoin rose to over $7,000, peaking at over $11,000 by mid-2019. The onset of the COVID-19 pandemic caused a mass adoption of Bitcoin and other cryptocurrencies. The price of Bitcoin soared between October 2019 and December 2020, from about $10,000 to over $20,000 per bitcoin. By 2021, businesses, banks, and institutional and retail investors had begun to invest in Bitcoin, causing its price to skyrocket to over $35,000 by January 2021 and surpass $60,000 in March 2021. Bitcoin experienced its highest recorded price in April 2021: $64,000.

The rollercoaster continued as Bitcoin's price crashed to $40,000 in September 2021, only to rise above $60,000 again in mid-October.[34] Billionaire PayPal co-founder Peter Thiel observed that Bitcoin's recent price surges "surely tells us that we are at a complete bankruptcy moment for the central banks."[35]

4. THE TOTAL CIRCULATION AND SUPPLY OF BITCOIN

If the U.S. government prints more money, the value of the dollar decreases. Just think what $100 could buy two decades ago compared to today. Bitcoin is different.

There are about 18.8 million bitcoins in circulation, with this number increasing as mining continues. But the Bitcoin supply is limited to 21 million Bitcoins, and miners have already extracted about 89.7% of

34. COINMARKETCAP, *Bitcoin,* coinmarketcap.com, (last visited Apr. 22, 2022).
35. THOMAS BARRABI, *Billionaire Peter Thiel Touts Bitcoin, Says He Is 'Underinvested,'* foxbusiness.com, (Oct. 21, 2021).

bitcoins.[36] Once miners have mined 21 million bitcoins (estimated to occur in 2140), the supply maximum will be reached.

The computer nodes that make up the blockchain network enforce Nakamoto's "hard cap" on the Bitcoin supply by using the source code.[37] Theoretically, the source code could be altered to increase the supply of bitcoins available, but that would require a consensus decision to implement a new version of the source code with a higher cap. Each node in the network either adopts the change or is forced off the network (a process known as a "hard fork"). Achieving that level of consensus is difficult and requires collaboration between several groups, many of which have an incentive to keep Bitcoin scarce.

Bitcoin undergoes a "halving" event every four years, which reduces the number of bitcoins rewarded for every block that is mined. The last halving occurred on May 11, 2020 and reduced the reward from 12.5 to 6.25 bitcoins. The next halving will occur in the spring of 2024.

Bitcoin operates as a deflationary currency, like gold. There is a finite amount of gold on earth; it is neither made nor created. As individuals mine more gold, it becomes harder to find other gold locations, and the entrance of gold into the economy decreases. This scarcity increases the demand for gold, just like Bitcoin. Whereas the demand for gold has continued for generations, questions persist as to whether the demand for Bitcoin will continue, particularly as new cryptocurrencies enter the market.

SUMMARY

Bitcoin has established itself as a valuable and minable source of wealth. Unlike gold, Bitcoin is mined with computers algorithms. Bitcoin's scarcity can increase its value over time, but it has a volatile price history. Today, almost 19 million bitcoins are in circulation with a combined market value of over a trillion U.S. dollars. As Bitcoin has grown in popularity, other cryptocurrencies have emerged.

36. BITCOINBLOCKHALF, *Bitcoin Block Reward Halving Countdown*, bitcoinblockhalf.com, (last visited Apr. 22, 2022).

37. SATOSHI NAKAMOTO, *Bitcoin: A Peer-to-Peer Electronic Cash System*, (2008).

§ 4 Other Cryptocurrencies

There are over 6,000 cryptocurrencies today.[38] This number is expected to grow as more users accept cryptocurrencies as a form of value—whether to trade or invest. Along with brokers and exchanges that help individuals invest in cryptocurrencies, online payment companies such as PayPal are allowing users to buy, sell, and hold four cryptocurrencies: Bitcoin, Ethereum, Litecoin, and Bitcoin Cash.[39]

1. EXAMPLES

Cryptocurrencies that started after Bitcoin are known as "Altcoins." Altcoins can include other cryptocurrencies, tokens (virtual asset or utility), and stablecoins (cryptos with their price pegged to a stable asset).[40]

- **Ethereum (ETH):** Programmer Vitalik Buterin developed Ethereum as a decentralized software platform with several advantages over Bitcoin. For instance, Ethereum allows the execution of smart contracts on its platform without third-party interference. Ethereum's goal is to allow anyone access to its decentralized package of financial products. The platform's token is called "Ether." In 2021, Ethereum transitioned its algorithm from proof-of-work to proof-of-stake to enable Ethereum to operate with less energy and greater transaction speed. As of 2021, Ethereum's market capitalization (current market value of the cryptocurrency)

---

38. COINMARKETCAP, *Cryptocurrencies,* coinmarketcap.com, (last visited Apr. 22, 2022).
39. STEPHEN MCBRIDE, *You Can Now Buy Bitcoin on PayPal for $1,* forbes.com, (2020).
40. LUKE CONWAY, *Most Important Cryptocurrencies Other Than Bitcoin,* investopedia.com, (2016).

was about $441.3 billion.[41] Billionaire entrepreneur Mark Cuban commented, "Ethereum is really a significant network, and because of their smart contracts and their security and their ability to have distributed management, I think you're going to see a lot of unique business applications occur."[42]

- **Binance Coin (BNB):** Binance Coin is a utility token (a coin unique to the ecosystem that allows users to participate in certain limited activities on the network) that relies on proof-of-stake consensus. Individuals receive discounts on the Binance Exchange if they use Binance Coin to pay their fees. Binance Coin has the third-largest market capitalization in the world at about $79.2 billion in late 2021.[43]
- **Cardano (ADA):** Cardano is a proof-of-stake cryptocurrency created by a group of engineers and mathematicians. It was co-founded by one of the founding members of the Ethereum project, Charles Hoskinson, who had dissented with some of Ethereum's properties. Cardano was established based on five principles: people, purpose, technology, research, and opportunity.[44] The platform creates a decentralized financial package that solves multiple objectives, including contract tracing. Cardano has the fourth-largest market capitalization at about $71 billon.[45]
- **Tether (USDT):** Tether was one of the first "stablecoins." Stablecoins are like cryptocurrencies but base their market value on some external source to reduce price volatility. Tether is unique because its price correlates with the U.S. dollar, allowing for efficient transfers from other cryptocurrencies to the U.S. dollar (via Tether). This reduction of volatility is significant because other cryptocurrencies—including Bitcoin—experience drastic, unpredictable price fluctuations. Tether had the fifth-highest market capitalization at about $68.5 billion as of mid-October 2021.[46]

---

41. COINMARKETCAP, *Ethereum,* coinmarketcap.com, (last visited Apr. 22, 2022).
42. BRECK DUMAS, *Mark Cuban Explains How 'Not All Crypto is the Same',* foxbusiness.com, (Oct. 4, 2021).
43. COINMARKETCAP, *Binance Coin,* coinmarketcap.com, (last visited Apr. 22, 2022).
44. CARDANO, *Discover Cardano,* Cardano.org.com, (last visited Apr. 22, 2022).
45. COINMARKETCAP, *Cardano,* coinmarketcap.com, (last visited Apr. 22, 2022).
46. COINMARKETCAP, *Tether,* coinmarketcap.com, (last visited Apr. 22, 2022).

- **Polkadot (DOT):** Polkadot is a proof-of-stake cryptocurrency that enables interoperability between different blockchains. This interoperability is important because it facilitates cooperation by connecting multiple permissioned and permissionless blockchains. As of mid-October 2021, it had a market capitalization of about $40.1 billion.[47]
- **Chainlink (LINK):** Chainlink is a decentralized oracle network (a service that connects smart contracts on the Ethereum network to information) built on the Ethereum Blockchain that facilitates the transfer of data to smart-contract applications. Chainlink solves the problem of blockchains' inability to connect securely to real-world data by allowing smart contracts to communicate with outside input. Its token is called "LINK." As of mid-October 2021, the market capitalization of Chainlink was about $12.3 billion.[48]
- **Litecoin (LTC):** Litecoin was created by former Google engineer and MIT graduate Charlie Lee as an open-source global payment system that operates without third-party or government interference. Litecoin has a faster block-generation rate than Bitcoin, meaning that it also has faster transaction-confirmation times. Litecoin had a market capitalization of almost $12.2 billion as of mid-October 2021.[49]
- **Bitcoin Cash (BCH):** Bitcoin Cash (BCH) launched in 2017 as a successful "hard fork" from Bitcoin. A fork occurs where miners and developers reach multiple disagreements about an issue and decide to split the cryptocurrency into two chains. The first chain is the original code (Bitcoin), and the second chain contains several new changes to the code (Bitcoin Cash). Bitcoin Cash held a market capitalization of almost $11.2 billion in mid-October 2021.[50]
- **Stellar (XLM):** Stellar is a blockchain network that aims to provide large-scale enterprise solutions for processing large transactions at low cost without intermediaries. Stellar's cryptocurrency is called "Lumens." Stellar had a market capitalization of about $8.8 billion as of mid-October 2021.[51]

---

47. COINMARKETCAP, *Polkadot,* coinmarketcap.com, (last visited Apr. 22, 2022).
48. COINMARKETCAP, *Chainlink,* coinmarketcap.com, (last visited Apr. 22, 2022).
49. COINMARKETCAP, *Litecoin,* coinmarketcap.com, (last visited Apr. 22, 2022).
50. COINMARKETCAP, *Bitcoin Cash*, coinmarketcap.com, (last visited Apr. 22, 2022).
51. COINMARKETCAP, *Stellar Lumens,* coinmarketcap.com, (last visited Apr. 22, 2022).

- **Monero (XMR):** Monero is an untraceable, decentralized cryptocurrency that has received widespread support because of its privacy-enhancing capabilities. Monero's security, privacy, and anonymity have earned it a notorious reputation for its ability to facilitate online global criminal schemes. In mid-October 2021, its market capitalization stood at about $4.8 billion.[52]

2. CRYPTO ASSETS

The term "crypto asset" includes crypto commodities, cryptocurrencies, and crypto securities. Crypto commodities include economic goods, services, and fungible derivatives. The producer does not matter to the market. Cryptocurrencies are the representations of U.S. currency or synthetic derivatives on blockchain technology. Crypto securities refer to all debt and equity that uses blockchain technology.

In early 2020, Representative Paul Gosar introduced H.R.6154—Cryptocurrency Act of 2020, which seeks to "clarify which [f]ederal agencies regulate digital assets, to require those agencies to notify the public of any federal licenses, certifications, or registrations required to create or trade in such assets . . ."

The bill (a) divides crypto assets into three categories: (1) crypto commodities, (2) cryptocurrencies, and (3) cryptosecurities; and (b) proposes that different federal authorities regulate these three categories: (i) the Commodity Futures Trading Commission (CFTC) would govern crypto commodities, (ii) the Financial Crimes Enforcement Network, cryptocurrencies; and (iii) the SEC, crypto securities. The bill evidences the United States' progress in becoming the global leader of cryptocurrencies and its attempts to make it easier for businesses, institutions, and individuals to participate in the growing crypto industry without the current uncertainty.[53]

SUMMARY

Cryptocurrencies continue to flourish with no apogee in sight. Despite attempts at regulation, cryptocurrencies continue to enjoy a shadowy existence that further contributes to its poriferous status of value and wealth. While many people are dithyrambic supporters of a new decentralized asset, others display more aversion, in part because of ongoing reports of criminals usurping cryptocurrencies to operate outside of government oversight.

---

52. COINMARKETCAP, *Monero,* coinmarketcap.com, (last visited Apr. 22, 2022).
53. KEVIN HELMS, *U.S. Lawmaker Introduces Crypto-Currency Act of 2020 While Under Coronavirus Quarantine,* bitcoin.com, (2020).

§ 5 Tokenization

Tokenization is converting tangible assets or non-physical assets into tokens by using blockchain technology. Tokenization has a place and function within all industries, whether traditional industries such as real estate, debt and equity, collectibles, and artwork, or novel industries such as play-to-earn games or De-Fi. An individual or company's goals dictate the type of assets to be tokenized and the kind of token to issue to others.

1. COINS VS. TOKENS

People often use the terms coin and token interchangeably. Yet they do not mean the same thing in the crypto and blockchain spheres.

A "coin" refers to a digital form of money that is created to act as a payment method (for example, Bitcoin). Crypto coins are bought, sold, traded, converted into other cryptocurrencies, or exchanged for fiat currencies. These types of coins use blockchain technology—often their own blockchain. Bitcoin uses the Bitcoin Blockchain, Litecoin uses the Litecoin Blockchain, Ether uses the Ethereum Blockchain, and Monero uses the Monero Blockchain.

A "token" is a digital representation of an asset. Tokens do not have the same "money" purpose as cryptocurrency. Rather, a token represents an ownership interest or serves a specific function. Tokens often rely on the Ethereum Blockchain—which introduced tokens—or on another coin's blockchain.

2. THREE MAIN TYPES OF TOKENS

There are three main types of tokens, classified based on their function and purpose: (1) security tokens, (2) utility tokens, and (3) non-fungible tokens (NFTs).

Security Tokens. Security tokens are like traditional securities (for example, shares or bonds) and represent an ownership interest embodied as a crypto token—a digital company share. The SEC views security tokens as a "security" for registration purposes under the federal securities laws.[54]

Utility Tokens. Utility tokens serve only one function, and their issuance depends on that designated purpose. Think of them as a casino chip or arcade token—individuals can use these tokens for the purpose of the issuance. Supply and demand drive these tokens' price.[55]

NFTs. NFTs are unique digital assets that individuals can buy and trade and represent the most common kind of tokenization. Tokens can be fungible, meaning they can be replaced, or non-fungible, meaning they are unique and cannot be replicated. Individuals use fungible tokens just like currencies for transactions. An example is Bitcoin. One bitcoin equals the next bitcoin. Non-fungible tokens, or NFTs, on the other hand, are unique digital assets. NFTs are "tokenized." They serve as a digital certificate of ownership for both virtual and real-world assets that can be bought and sold. A public blockchain stores the NFT purchase, which serves as evidence of ownership of the one-of-a-kind NFT. Individuals and companies offer tokens through either an ICO or a newer form—a Security Token Offering (STO).

But what do purchasers gain from buying a digitized asset? Imagine you want to purchase an NFT of LeBron James's slam dunk. Anyone can view pictures of his slam dunks on Google; why purchase an NFT? The answer lies in knowing that you are the only one with the official and genuine version of the NFT. Buyers receive a certificate of ownership that preserves the NFT's value. Without this immutable proof of ownership, the asset is worthless.

It's the same as collecting antique sports cards. Such a collection's value is defined by its authenticity, the worth to the owner, and its uniqueness and rarity. The NFT marketplace is no different. Whether acquired as a collectible or investment, NFTs are genuine. An individual can resell, trade, or keep them as a memory of a personal experience. Thus, individuals are paying for exclusivity, rarity, and authenticity, which gives the NFT as much value as the individual is willing to attach to it. The more value an NFT has, the more expensive it is. The blockchain stores the NFT purchases, and no one can alter the blockchain. This assures fans that their NFT purchases are safe from tampering or theft.

NFTs have been taking the world by storm. Around May 2021, the NFT market capitalization stood at $17.9 billion. Just a few months later

---

54. CAROL GOFORTH, *Securities Treatment of Tokenized Offerings under U.S. Law,* 46 Pepp. L. Rev. 405, (2019).
55. JONATHAN ROHR & AARON WRIGHT, *Blockchain-Based Token Sales, Initial Coin Offerings, and the Democratization of Public Capital Markets,* 70 Hastings L.J. 463, (2019).

in October 2021, it grew to $27.18 billion.[56] The NFT market generated significant attention when an NFT created by digital artist Beeple—a collage called "Everydays: The First 5000 Days"—sold for a striking $69 million.[57] The NBA Top Shot—an NFT marketplace where users can buy, sell, and collect NBA memories and moments—has become one of the biggest NFT successes to date. As Top Shot creates more curiosity for memorable basketball moments, sports enthusiasts and fans have joined the NFT bandwagon.[58]

3. ICOS VS. STOS

Individuals and companies use ICOs and STOs for fundraising, and both use blockchain technology. ICOs developed first and allow anyone in the world to launch a project by offering tokens in exchange for investor funds or crypto payments. STOs tend to conform to federal regulatory requirements and offer more protection to investors. Though anyone with the necessary tech and product can launch an ICO, issuers must back the tokens offered in an STO with something of value, such as company assets. STOs are unavailable to all investors but are more trustworthy than ICOs. Think of STOs as a tokenized crowdfunding sale compliant with SEC rules and regulations. The objective of an STO is to continue blockchain crowdfunding offers of ICOs, but with more investor protection and the SEC's seal of approval.[59]

4. SECURITY TOKENS VS. TRADITIONAL SECURITIES

The SEC treats security tokens just like traditional securities—as ownership interests. Both need registration as a security offering or an applicable registration exemption, and both must comply with various disclosure and reporting obligations. If there is uncertainty on whether a security token is a security, the SEC will analyze whether the token qualifies as an "investment contract."

But what is the difference between a traditional security and a digital security token? A traditional security is any representation of an ownership interest in a publicly traded entity. It is an investment contract that individuals can resell and trade on the secondary market. A digital security—or security token—is a digitally issued online representation

56. COINCODEX, *NFT Tokens by Market Cap and Volume,* coincodex.com, (last visited Apr. 22, 2022).
57. JACOB KASTRENAKES, *Beeple sold an NFT for $69 million,* theverge.com, (Mar. 11, 2021).
58. NBATOPSHOT, *Own the NBA's Best Plays*, nbatopshot.com, (last visited Apr. 22, 2022).
59. THOMAS LAMBERT et al., *Security Token Offerings,* SMALL BUSINESS ECONOMICS, (2021).

of an asset. These digital assets can represent equity, real estate, investment contracts, company shares, and commodities. The main difference is that the blockchain stores ownership proof of the security tokens.

Another difference involves the type of issuer. Publicly traded companies offer traditional securities and register and list them on U.S. stock exchanges, allowing the public to invest in their securities at any time. Private entities issue security tokens, and these tokens may not need to be registered on a stock exchange. Blockchain technology allows anyone to purchase a security token. Thus, these security tokens offer start-ups greater access to capital and present fewer entry barriers to investing.

5. SECURITY TOKENS VS. UTILITY TOKENS

Private entities offer both security and utility tokens. A big difference between security and utility tokens is value expectation. The value of a security token corresponds to the company's value. If the company's value increases, the value of its tokens will also increase. Security tokens are clear examples of securities under the federal securities laws.

While a security token represents legal ownership of a digital asset, utility tokens entitle purchasers to use the token for the specific purpose outlined in its issuance. The value of utility tokens has no (direct) relation to the value of the company. Another significant difference is federal regulation. Unlike security tokens, there is little—if any—regulation for utility token ICOs. This lack of utility-token regulation means a higher risk of fraud and scams than with security tokens.

SUMMARY

Fungible and non-fungible tokens are the next step of blockchain technology. Examples like Beeple and NBA Top Shot have highlighted how NFTs can generate value. As individuals become more experienced with tokens, they are now issued in ICOs or STOs—depending on their purpose, function, and use.

§ 6 Artificial Intelligence (AI)

Artificial intelligence (AI) started gaining attention in the 1950s to streamline cumbersome, repetitive tasks and reduce production costs. From virtual agents and automated financial assistance to online mapping, speech recognition, and facial recognition, AI is now ubiquitous in our daily lives.

But less is known about AI's role in trading. The AI marketplace is complex with multiple, ever-changing variables that make it unpredictable—the Bitcoin price rollercoaster is a prime example. Yet companies continue to invest in AI in hopes of predicting and capitalizing on the market's twists and turns.

1. AI AND TRADING

The complexity of financial-market prediction has led companies to develop statistical models with decision-making capabilities that rely on AI. Applying AI to financial-market prediction involves automated processes that recognize patterns in trading activity, consume those patterns, and make an appropriate decision accordingly.

The information that the AI system consumes and analyzes is the same data and patterns that humans use when taking stock-market actions.[60] The main difference with AI analysis is the lack of human judgment in its decision-making processes. Whereas humans may overlook subtle details and make irrational, emotional, or subjective decisions, AI systems can recognize and act on patterns in real time without the hindrance of these "human" factors.

Another key difference is speed. A computer can process greater amounts of data than a human and can do so in seconds.

---

60. FERNANDO G.D.C. FERREIRA et al., *Artificial Intelligence Applied to Stock Market Trading: A Review,* 9 IEEE ACCESS 30898–30917, (2021).

2. THE INCREASED RELIANCE ON MACHINE LEARNING

Capital market firms are using AI to build complex algorithm systems that can "learn" from data and predict certain outcomes. But how do machines learn?

Machine learning is a type of AI designed to help software applications learn how to make decisions. The process involves inputting large amounts of data into an algorithm so that the application can make decisions and then learn from prior inputted data without manual programming.[61]

Machine learning has become a popular tool in predicting financial market activity and has disrupted traditional trading practices. But its success depends on the quality of the inputted data. Machine learning depends on finding preexisting relationships between inputs and the software's output. If there is no relationship between the inputted and outputted variables, the prediction will be wrong.[62]

3. ADVANTAGES AND DISADVANTAGES OF AI IN TRADING

The chief advantage of AI in trading is the elimination of emotions. AI relies solely on the evaluation of inputs. There is no room for subjectivity or individual interpretation. As a result, the use of AI eliminates differences among individuals.

The automation of AI trading systems also provides more efficiencies. AI executes orders as soon as certain trading conditions occur. The automation element is beneficial for cryptocurrency investments. Unlike the stock market, crypto markets never close. With AI, you can go to sleep knowing that your crypto order will execute—including any stop-loss orders.

AI comes with several disadvantages. If an AI system is set up on a computer (rather than a server), a poor internet connection can prevent trade orders from reaching the market and executing. AI systems also need continuous monitoring to avoid order glitches and processing mistakes, for example, accidental duplication of a trade order.[63]

61. NOAH MITSUHASHI, *How AI Will Democratize Access to Investing,* forbes.com, (2021).
62. SHIVAM SINHA, *Making Machine Learning Work for Financial Market Predictions,* forbes.com, (2021).
63. JEAN FOLGER, *Automated Trading Systems: The Pros and Cons,* investopedia.com, (2019).

Despite these disadvantages, AI has played—and will continue to play—a pivotal role in the development of digital currencies and blockchain technology.

4. DEEP LEARNING

Deep learning is a specialized branch of machine learning that trains computers to learn like humans—through experience. In the computer world, experience is data. Deep learning works by feeding the system with large data sets (such as pixel data, audio files, or text data documents) and using multiple processing layers to classify the data by diverse features.

For example, imagine we supply a deep-learning system with millions of images of dogs. Using this large data set, the machine classifies the pixels that contain representations of a dog's features. The machine can then independently learn what groups of features denote a dog in the image.[64]

a. How Deep Learning Works

Deep learning uses neural networks computing systems that mimic the biological brain via algorithms to simulate human decision-making processes faster and more accurately.

Imagine you are looking at an image composed of fifty million pixels, and you must locate a picture of a house in the image. It would take you a long time to find it. Before deep learning, individuals would program a machine to search for individual house parts—for example, a window or a roof. But there are several types of window and roofs, so this was not an ideal approach. Deep learning relies on a pool of data (millions of home images) and complex algorithms that enable the machine to learn what features to look for to identify a home. The system learns to identify homes using the entire data pool rather than being limited to the specific data inputted by a human.

It is more efficient for the system to learn by itself rather than rely on human design and input. Deep learning generates results faster and with more accuracy. It is a more focused and sophisticated form of machine learning.[65]

---

64. YANN LECUN et al., *Deep learning,* 521 NATURE 436–444, (2015).
65. BO ZHOU, *Deep Learning and the Cross-Section of Stock Returns: Neural Networks Combining Price and Fundamental Information*, (2019).

b. Deep Learning's Impact in Finance and Trading

A new area of research focuses on whether deep-learning strategies can be applied to finance and market prediction. Consider hedge funds or investment banks that engage in arbitrage strategies. Statistical arbitrage is an investment strategy that uses temporal price differences between similar assets. The success of this strategy depends on the asset portfolios, their temporary price deviations, and how trading could optimize the result of the trade. Machine learning using neural networks can optimally solve these complex arbitrage prediction issues because neural networks—deep-learning techniques—can learn the arbitrage signals and make a trading allocation.[66]

Deep learning may also be useful with stock-market movements. Deep learning can work with nonlinear equations and examine neural networks containing public market data. Research suggests that deep-learning systems can help with stock price predictions, financial decision-making, and analysis of a particular stock's price movement.[67]

Deep learning has been a major AI breakthrough for analyzing complex audio, video, speech, and pixel files, and has played an integral role in several industries. Machines can now autonomously review data and reach a solution, providing more possibilities for finance and trading.

SUMMARY

Some examples of specialized AI applications include machine learning and deep learning. While these processes rely on different methods, they provide similar results, such as objectivity and efficiency in stock-market operations, trading, and investments. AI could revolutionize many industries by emulating—but optimizing—the analysis of the savviest human experts.

66. JORGE GUIJARRO-ORDONEZ et al., *Deep Learning Statistical Arbitrage*, (2021).

67. NABIPOUR et al., *Deep Learning for Stock Market Prediction,* 22 ENTROPY 8, (2020).

§ 7 Government Positions

The current uncertainty about the regulatory status of cryptocurrencies will end—in the United States and elsewhere. Cryptocurrencies are too much of a fiscal reality to ignore. Each economic crisis (for example, the COVID-19 market crash, fiat-currency inflation, and economic depression) has catapulted non-fiat assets to the front of people's minds. Attempts to regulate are bipartisan, making cryptocurrencies an apolitical, beguiling opportunity to find consensus across party lines.

There are three conceivable regulatory models: (1) prohibit decentralized currencies combined with a state-controlled monopolization of digital assets (China), (2) elevate decentralized currencies to the rank of official government payment forms (El Salvador), or (3) a combination of (1) and (2). No matter the approach, governments will have to recognize and accept the perpetual existence of cryptocurrencies and its underlying blockchain technology.

1. THE UNITED STATES

Federal agencies, including the SEC, CFTC, Department of Justice (DOJ), and Internal Revenue Service (IRS), have taken an interest in companies that use blockchain technology or offer cryptocurrencies to the public, as well as companies and individuals that engage in criminal activity involving cryptocurrencies. Common examples of crypto-related fraud include crypto laundering, illegally layering crypto transactions into multiple wallets, illegal conversion of cryptos to fiat currencies, fraudulent ICOs, and tax fraud involving crypto-related activities. Former FBI Supervisory Special Agent Kevin Sheridan notes:

> Similar to traditional money laundering techniques involving the moving of cash though various legitimate and shell accounts, criminals exploit cryptocurrencies use anonymizing services to hide

> the source of the funds and break the links between digital currency transactions.

The government investigates both intentional and inadvertent failures to follow the law. Companies using blockchain technology, crypto exchanges, and those offering crypto as an investment need to make sure they are complying with all applicable laws and regulations, including the Bank Secrecy Act and its stringent Know Your Customer (KYC) and Anti-Money Laundering (AML) regulations. Entities and individuals also need to make sure that their offerings do not constitute securities under federal law (unless they are prepared to take the steps necessary to comply with the law) and that they properly report their crypto transactions to the IRS. Failure to meet these requirements may have devastating consequences.

The DOJ has initiated a plethora of investigations for crypto fraud. In early September 2021, the U.S. Attorney for the Southern District of New York announced crypto investment fraud charges against individuals who had started a cryptocurrency investment fund that led to investor losses of more than $30 million. The DOJ alleged that the individuals used at least $9 millions of investor funds to make lavish personal purchases. In October 2021, the Acting U.S. Attorney for the Northern District of Texas announced that the founders of a crypto ICO had pleaded guilty to tax evasion after raising about $24 million from over 13,000 investors. The founders also admitted that they had used investor funds for personal expenses and purposely circumvented financial-reporting requirements.[68]

Criminals have turned to Bitcoin to carry out money laundering schemes. Bitcoin transactions are fast, easy, unregulated, and difficult to trace. Remember, the advent of Bitcoin led to the opening of the "Silk Road"—an online black market advertised on the dark web where individuals could buy illegal drugs and other illegal products using the seminal cryptocurrency.[69] Retired FBI Special Agent Kevin Sheridan adds:

> "As digital currency becomes more mainstream in daily business and investing transactions, it is certain criminals will further exploit bitcoin's blockchain systems to orchestrate complex money laundering and fraud schemes."

68. U.S. DEPARTMENT OF JUSTICE, News, *Founders of Crypto ICO Plead Guilty to Tax Evasion After Raising $24 Million from Investors*, (2021).
69. DAVID ADLER, *Silk Road: The Dark Side of Cryptocurrency*, news.law.fordham.edu, (21 Feb. 2018).

Federal agencies are using existing statutes to prosecute individuals suspected of using cryptocurrencies for illegal purposes. The IRS is investigating taxpayers who fail to report crypto transactions and is prosecuting individuals and companies for tax evasion and filing false returns. Other federal agencies are investigating entities for failing to implement compliance policies or maintain clear AML/KYC procedures under the Bank Secrecy Act. The SEC and CFTC are working with FINRA and FinCEN to analyze ICOs and refer cases to the Federal Bureau of Investigation (FBI) and DOJ when they find evidence of criminal activity.

> "Those who enter the arena of cryptocurrency must do so with an awareness that the treatment of the currency by regulators, government authorities and the markets remain subject to frequent and significant fluctuations and reevaluation." Marie Kondzielski, retired FBI Special Agent and Certified Fraud Examiner.

Among all areas of cryptocurrency fraud enforcement, fraudulent Bitcoin operations appear to be at the top of the list. In June 2021, the DOJ seized 63.7 bitcoins valued at about $2.3 million paid to DarkSide after its ransomware attack on Colonial Pipeline.[70] Also in June 2021, the U.S. Attorney for the Northern District of Texas announced a plea by "Doctor Bitcoin" for his illegal operation of a cash-to-crypto conversion business, which converted between $550,000 and $1.5 million to Bitcoin for a fee.[71]

Cryptocurrencies and blockchain technology are evolving into a force that some people argue cannot be stopped. Jeremy Allaire, co-founder, chair, and CEO of Circle Internet Financial, stated:

> [T]he technology of blockchains and digital assets are not standing still, and whatever the ultimate policy and regulatory outcomes, it is crucial that policy embraces and enables the United States to be global leaders in the development of the internet of value.[72]

A significant hurdle to mass crypto adoption in the United States remains the lack of user knowledge. As stated by Tim Allen, former U.S. Secret Service Senior Special Agent and certified digital forensics expert., "In many instances, one must be savvy enough to move their cryptocurrency from an exchange to a wallet, and sometimes to a third-party app to purchase something. Basically, it's not user friendly."

70. DOJ RELEASE, *Department of Justice Seizes $2.3 Million in Cryptocurrency Paid to the Ransomware Extortionists Darkside*, (2021).
71. DOJ RELEASE, *Doctor Bitcoin Pleads Guilty to Illegal Cash-to-Crypto Scheme*, (2021).
72. REV.COM, *Crypto CEOs Testify Before House Financial Services Hearing Transcript,* rev.com, (Dec. 8, 2021).

2. CHINA

China made international news when it banned financial institutions from conducting transactions in cryptocurrencies in 2013. They later extended this ban to cryptocurrency exchanges, banning all ICOs. The stated reason for the ban was that ICO activity facilitated public financing without approval from the Chinese government.

In May 2021, the chair of China's Financial Stability and Development Committee, Vice-Premier Liu He, stated that the Chinese government will "crack down on Bitcoin mining and trading behavior, and resolutely prevent the transfer of individual risks to the society."[73]

In November 2021, China banned crypto-mining operations from the country—contributing to a cryptocurrency mass sell-off. Mining companies are now facing strict requirements in China or being forced to relocate to jurisdictions with more favorable regulatory environments for miners.

In 2021, China introduced its own digital currency—called the e-yuan—which was classified to be "issued and regulated by the central bank and . . . guaranteed by the Chinese state."[74] Individuals can use the digital yuan both domestically and internationally.

3. EUROPEAN UNION

While each E.U. member state has its own framework and approach, a few trends are worth noting. For example, in September 2020, the European Commission released the draft Markets in Crypto-Assets Regulation (MiCA), which provides for enhanced consumer protections and treats cryptocurrency as a regulated financial instrument—thus subjecting cryptocurrency to regulatory oversight.

Taxation of crypto transactions varies depending on the country, and tax rates can range from zero to 50%. In January 2020, the E.U. released the Fifth Anti-Money Laundering Directive (AMLD5), which will "require crypto exchanges and custodial service providers to register with their local regulator and demonstrate compliance with thoroughgoing KYC and AML procedures."[75] In comparing U.S. and E.U. regulation of cryptocurrencies and blockchain technology, digital forensics expert Tim Allen stated:

---

73. IRIS DENG, *China to Crack Down on Mining of Cryptocurrencies, Delivering A One-Two Punch to Digital Tokens After Triggering Global Sell-Off,* finance.yahoo.com, (May 22, 2021).
74. JAMES KYNGE AND SUN YU, *Virtual Control: The Agenda Behind China's New Digital Currency,* ft.com, (Feb 16, 2021).
75. IAN ALLISON, *European Crypto Firms Brace for Higher Costs as AMLD5 Takes Effect,* coindesk.com, (Jan 10, 2020).

In the U.S., individual states have introduced their own rules and regulations because the federal government has not exercised its constitutional pre-emptive power to regulate blockchain. In 2020, the E.U. signed its fifth AML Directive into law which caused cryptocurrencies and services to fall under regulatory scrutiny. Thus, the E.U. is far ahead in regulating cryptocurrency when compared to the U.S.

4. GERMANY

German regulations provide that individuals and entities can only buy or trade crypto assets through licensed exchanges and custodians, including those licensed by the German Federal Financial Supervisory Authority (BaFin).

In January 2020, Germany implemented the AMLD5, emphasizing that crypto assets qualify as financial instruments and that providers of crypto custody services are financial institutions.[76] Crypto assets do not have the legal status of currency in Germany. Instead, they are considered a means of exchange or payment that individuals can trade, store, exchange, or transfer.

5. OTHER COUNTRIES

Other countries are also adapting to the evolving blockchain and crypto sphere. Canada, for instance, has strived to recognize and regulate the rise of cryptocurrencies, and it was the first country to approve a Bitcoin ETF in February 2021. Canada treats crypto assets as commodities for tax purposes, as they are not a recognized form of legal tender. Its main securities regulators—the Canadian Securities Administrators (CSA) and the Investment Industry Regulatory Organization of Canada (IIROC)—require crypto-trading platforms and dealers to register with provincial regulators.

In the United Kingdom, cryptocurrencies are treated as property and not as a form of legal tender. Online crypto exchanges must register with the U.K. Financial Conduct Authority (FCA). Crypto exchanges in the United Kingdom cannot offer crypto derivatives trading. In January 2021, the United Kingdom's Her Majesty's Treasury (HMT) initiated a consultation on crypto assets to ensure that the U.K. is, "equipped to harness the benefits of new technologies, propelling and boosting

---

76. HANS STAMM & DENISE BLESSING, *AMLD5 in Germany: Implementation Provides Far-Reaching Licensing Requirements for Crypto-Asset Service Providers*, eurekahedge.com, (Aug. 16, 2019).

innovation and competition, while mitigating risks to consumers and stability."[77]

In January 2020, the Commissione Nazionale per le Società e la Borsa (CONSOB)—the governmental entity responsible for regulating Italian financial markets—published a report on crypto assets, initial bids, and exchanges.[78] In September 2020, France's Autorité des Marchés Financiers (AMF) published a Q&A series discussing key issues on the digital asset service provider regime created under France's Plan for Business Growth and Transformation (PACTE).[79] PACTE establishes a legal framework for digital asset service providers.

In November 2020, Hong Kong's Financial Services and Treasury Bureau (FSTB) issued a Consultation Paper that proposed to, "enhance anti-money laundering and counter-terrorist financing ('AML/CTF') regulation in Hong Kong," by introducing licensing and registration regimes for virtual asset services providers.[80] In May 2020, Japan's Financial Services Agency of Japan (FSA) published final amendments to the Payment Services Act (PSA) and the Financial Instruments and Exchange Act (FIEA) that include extensive regulations for "crypto asset derivative transactions."[81] Russia's central bank governor, Elvira Nabiullina, has announced that digital currencies are the future of financial systems in the country,[82] and the Russian government has been working to develop a new regulatory framework for cryptocurrencies. Russia has also created its own cryptocurrency, the CryptoRuble, which is issued by the Central Bank of Russia.

El Salvador's position on cryptocurrencies is noteworthy. In June 2021, El Salvador President Nayib Bukele announced that Bitcoin would become legal tender in the country.[83] El Salvador became the first country to accept Bitcoin as a legal currency. This means that in El

---

77. HM TREASURY, *UK Regulatory Approach to Cryptoassets and Stablecoins: Consultation and Call for Evidence*, www.gov.uk, (Jan. 7, 2021).
78. CONSOB, *Initial Offers and Exchanges of Crypto-Assets Final Report,* consob.it, (Jan 2, 2020).
79. AMF, *Digital Assets: The AMF Describes its Requirements for DASP Registration or License*, amf-france.org, (Sep. 22, 2020).
80. FSTB, *Public Consultation on Legislative Proposals to Enhance Anti-Money Laundering and Counter-Terrorist Financing Regulation in Hong Kong* fstb.gov.hk, (last visited April 22, 2022).
81. IFLR, *Japan: Getting a grip,* iflr.com, (Jun. 23, 2020).
82. ABIGAIL NG, *Digital Currencies are the Future for Russia's Financial System, Central Bank Governor says,* cnbc.com, (Jun. 2, 2021).
83. ARJUN KHARPAL & MACKENZIE SIGALOS, *El Salvador Bought $21 Million of Bitcoin as it Becomes First Country to Make it a Legal Currency,* cnbc.com, (Sep. 7, 2021).

Salvador, Bitcoin is now accepted everywhere as payment for goods and services alongside the U.S. dollar. El Salvador has also announced plans to build the world's first "Bitcoin City" funded by Bitcoin bonds.[84]

SUMMARY

The United States and the European Union are positioning themselves at the forefront of crypto and blockchain regulation. Enforcement of prohibited uses of cryptocurrencies predates parliamentary elaboration of the permitted applications.

The SEC, IRS, DOJ, and law enforcement agencies throughout the E.U. have already been investigating and prosecuting individuals and companies for violating existing laws and regulations that apply to crypto transactions. Other countries are taking notable steps as well, though with varying aims and priorities. For example, while China has banned crypto-mining operations and established its own national cryptocurrency, other countries such as Germany and the United Kingdom are exploring ways to regulate the existing crypto markets and blockchain transactions.

Trading has changed its form, but not its purpose. All that is needed to trade are money, value, and trust. Blockchain technology has immense possibilities for business operations, financial planning, and individual investment. Its adoption may go mainstream with a triggering event—whether that event involves adoption of digital currencies by a central bank, payment systems in cryptocurrency, or government regulation. As society enters this new era in history, it will need lawyers to guide us on complex issues of blockchain technology and cryptocurrency regulation. Lawyers will be needed to assist in areas including crypto-fraud investigations, ICOs and security-token offerings, AML/KYC policies, tax-law compliance, due diligence, and more. What will come next is only limited by our imaginations.

84. NELSON RENTERIA, *El Salvador Plans First 'Bitcoin City,' Backed by Bitcoin Bonds*, REUTERS, (Nov. 22, 2021).

PART 2: LEGAL PRACTICE AREAS

"There is a new and exciting industry in the United States of cryptocurrency, whether Bitcoin or otherwise, that are generating jobs, entrepreneurs who are creating new values, new hedges against inflation, new opportunities, and it is fast moving. It is dynamic."

U.S. Senator Ted Cruz, Texas[85]

85. Press Release, Ted Cruz, U.S. Senator for Texas, *Sen. Cruz Leads Fight to Remove Harmful Regulations on Cryptocurrency from Wasteful Infrastructure Bill*, cruz.senate.gov, (Aug. 9, 2021).

§ 8 Smart Contracts

You are probably familiar with the basic definition of a contract: a legally enforceable agreement. For a more verbose definition, Black's Law Dictionary explains that a "contract" is "an agreement between two or more parties creating obligations that are enforceable or otherwise recognizable at law."[86] The concept that an agreement is "enforceable" against the parties is ancient and underlies fundamental aspects of modern society. The free-market economy, for example, could not function without enforceable contracts. And although businesses mainly use contracts, they also have cultural and political significance. Take marriage as an example. Marriage is a personal arrangement between two people, but it is also a contract with real, legal implications. Likewise, the theory of a "social contract" between the people that govern society and the governed is central to our political framework.

1. FROM THE PERSONAL AND BUSINESS CONTRACT TO THE SMART CONTRACT – INTRODUCTION

The average person will enter many contracts in their lifetime. These range from simple contracts, like ordering a cup of coffee, to complex contracts, like taking out a second mortgage on your house. With most simple contracts, confirming that the other party performed its obligations is simple. But with more complex contracts, such as insurance agreements or real estate sales, it can be harder to determine whether the parties have performed their obligations. This is especially true if various third parties are involved.

- Simple Personal Contract Example: Janet orders a cup of coffee. After she pays for the coffee, Janet knows that the coffee shop has performed its obligation once the barista calls her name and places her coffee on the pick-up counter. But, if Janet's name is not called and no coffee appears, she will know that the barista

86. "Contract," Black's Law Dictionary, (9th ed., 2009).

has forgotten to make her drink. In such cases, Janet can either demand a refund or, more likely, remind them that she ordered a coffee about ten minutes ago. If necessary, Janet can also prove that she held up her side of the bargain by showing her receipt.

- Complex Personal Contract Example: Bill is buying a home from Sharon. Both Bill and Sharon have their own real-estate agents. Once Bill and Sharon agree on a purchase price, the escrow agent collects the documents and coordinates closing. Bill gives a 40% down payment but needs to finance the rest, so he applies for a loan and communicates with financial institutions and lenders. Sharon does not have a financial background to understand the loan terms, so she hires an attorney and financial adviser to help her.

Matters are different in the world of business. In the business world, contracts can be so intricate that whole teams of lawyers must formulate, negotiate, and understand the terms of the agreement. Confirming that the parties to the contract are performing their obligations is even harder, even if the parties are freely sharing information.

- Business Contract Example: InvestBox, Co. is an investment-management company that offers investment-portfolio management and makes financial recommendations. Nancy's business operates in the financial industry and wants to hire someone who can manage buying and selling securities on the company's behalf. InvestBox and Nancy's business enter into a complex investment-management agreement that details the terms of when Nancy's business will provide funds for InvestBox to make investment strategies, the types of services InvestBox may undertake, and the management service fees Nancy's business must pay to InvestBox.

Reducing the uncertainty of traditional contract making is one of the main purposes of a smart contract. Smart contracts aim to simplify observation and verification of a party's performance by incorporating the contract terms into a computer program. Upon performance, the computer program will execute on its own. By combining this program with blockchain technology, performance of the contract becomes automatic, tamper proof, secure, and transparent.[87]

- Basic "Smart Contract-Like" Example: Carol is standing in front of a vending machine, about to purchase a snack. He looks at the items available, thinks about what he's in the mood for, and picks.

87. MATTHEW N.O. SADIKU, KELECHI G. EZE, & SARHAN M. MUSA, *Smart Contracts: A Primer*, 5 JOURNAL OF SCIENTIFIC AND ENGINEERING RESEARCH 538 (2018).

Once he knows what he wants, he puts money into the machine, presses the right number, and the machine dispenses his chosen delicious treat. Simple enough, right? When Carol provides the right input (money and pressing the right number), the machine provides the guaranteed output (his snack). The simple logic behind the vending machine's operation is as follows:

MONEY + SNACK SELECTION = SNACK DISPENSED

A smart contract works in the same manner. It is a computer program with certain protocols stating what to do *if* a given action takes place. Like a vending machine, a smart contract has logic programmed into it. When someone enters the right inputs into the smart contract, the program automatically dispenses outputs.

2. COINING THE TERM "SMART CONTRACTS"

Despite their roots in the ancient concept of contracts, smart contracts are an invention. And contrary to popular perception, they are not traditional contracts. The term "smart contracts" was first coined by Nick Szabo, a computer scientist, legal scholar, and cryptographer, in the early 1990s. Szabo was also one of the first people to suggest a decentralized digital currency and designed a mechanism for such a currency in 1998 that he called "bit gold." Although no one ever implemented bit gold, many recognized it as a precursor to the bitcoin protocol later implemented by the pseudonymous Satoshi Nakamoto.[88] Szabo originally defined a smart contract as "a set of promises, specified in digital form, including protocols within which the parties perform on these promises."[89] Szabo envisioned the embedding of contractual clauses directly into the world, whether via hardware or software, to make it prohibitively expensive to breach the contract.

Recall the vending-machine example. Szabo suggested that a vending machine is "the primitive ancestor of smart contracts."[90] The machine accepts money and dispenses the product. Ideally, the cost of breaking into the machine should be higher than the value of cash or product that the machine contains. Smart contracts, Szabo proposed, could embed contractual provisions into all sorts of property that is valuable and governed by digital means. Like the vending machine, a smart contract works by following a logical system written directly into computer code. This logic consists of simple statements: ***"if/when X occurs, then do Y."*** Using modern developments and innovation in cryptography, this

88. SHARMA, R., *Bit gold,* investopedia.com (Oct. 24, 2021).
89. NICK SZABO, *Smart Contracts: Building Blocks for Digital Markets* at 1, fon.hum.uva.nl, (2021).
90. *Id.*

computer code can be written directly into a blockchain. A network of computers then executes the actions (the doing of the ***Y***) when predetermined conditions occur and verify (the occurrence of the ***X***). These actions can include the releasing of funds, registering a vehicle, sending a notification, or issuing a ticket.[91] Although modern smart contracts use a blockchain, other platforms might host them as well.

Cryptographic protocols implement smart contracts with high levels of observability, verifiability, and enforceability.[92] Once the protocols execute, the blockchain updates, and no one can alter or reverse the result. To make smart contracts even more secure, only parties that have been granted access to the transaction may observe the results. By storing smart-contract data on a shared ledger, it becomes almost impossible to lose, or falsify, the information.

3. SMART CONTRACTS TODAY

Today, the term smart contract describes computer code, stored on a blockchain-based platform, that executes all or part of an agreement.[93] The most popular smart-contract platform is the Ethereum network—the second most used cryptocurrency platform.[94] Ethereum is also the largest open-ended decentralized software platform.[95] Since the Ethereum Blockchain launched in 2015, the term smart contracts has been applied to the concept of general-purpose computations that take place on a blockchain or distributed ledger. The U.S. National Institute of Standards and Technology, for example, describes a smart contract as a "collection of code and data (sometimes referred to as functions and state) that is deployed using cryptographically signed transactions on the blockchain network."[96] This definition extends beyond our traditional notion of a contract and can include any kind of computer program executed on a blockchain network.

---

91. IBM. *What are Smart Contracts on Blockchain?* ibm.com, (Last visited Nov. 24, 2021).
92. NICK SZABO, *Smart Contracts: Building Blocks for Digital Markets* at 4, fon.hum.uva.nl, (2021).
93. STUART D. LEVI & ALEX LIPTON, *An Introduction to Smart Contracts and their Potential and Inherent Limitations* at 1, The Harvard Law School Forum on Corporate Governance, corpgov.law.harvard.edu, (May 26, 2018).
94. NATHAN REIFF, *Bitcoin vs. Ethereum: What's the Difference?* investopedia.com, (Feb. 21, 2022).
95. *Id.*
96. DYLAN YAGA et al., *Blockchain Technology Overview, National Institute of Standards and Technology Internal/Interagency Report 8202* at 54, (2018).

Before discussing the benefits, risks, and uses of smart contracts, let's understand how smart contracts function. Below is a simplified presentation of drafting a smart contract:

- **First Step:** The parties to the smart contract must agree on the parameters of their agreement and reduce those parameters to a computer program. These are the rules of the smart contract and can be anything the parties agree upon.

- **Second Step:** Once the parties agree and implement the program onto a blockchain network, the code of the smart contract replicates across multiple nodes of the blockchain.[97] This provides the security, permanence, and immutability for which blockchain is renowned.[98] The replication also means that when a new block adds to the blockchain, the code executes.

- **Last Step:** Finally, if one of the parties can show that a parameter occurred, the code will execute the step that the revealed parameter (the occurrence of the ***X***) triggers. If there is no indication of completion, the code will not execute.[99]

Although the code may be the sole manifestation of the parties' agreement, it will complement a traditional, text-based contract and be used to execute certain provisions within the broader agreement. This is usually the case because, for the smart contract to function, the input parameters and execution steps need to be objective.[100] The actual tasks that smart contracts may perform (the doing of the ***Y***) tend to be rudimentary, such as transferring funds or issuing digital notifications. The inputs that the program can receive (the occurrence of the ***X***) are also simple and must be intelligible to the program. As blockchain technology becomes more prevalent, smart contracts will become more complex and will handle sophisticated transactions. Developers have already begun stringing together multiple transaction steps to form complex smart contracts. Because legal criteria can be subjective, it will be some time before smart contracts can determine, for example, whether a party exercised "reasonable care" or made "commercially reasonable" efforts.

A transaction fee is also required. Most blockchains require fees before the contract adds to the chain and executes. The Ethereum Blockchain,

97. STUART D. LEVI & ALEX LIPTON, *An Introduction to Smart Contracts and their Potential and Inherent Limitations* at 1, The Harvard Law School Forum on Corporate Governance, corpgov.law.harvard.edu, (May 26, 2018).
98. *Id.*
99. *Id.*
100. *Id.*

for example, executes smart contracts on the Ethereum Virtual Machine, or EVM.[101] The EVM is a blockchain-based software platform that allows developers to create decentralized applications. To add a contract to the Ethereum Blockchain, the parties must pay a fee of Ether cryptocurrency. This payment is known as "gas."[102] If the smart contract is complex and involves multiple transaction steps, an individual must pay more gas to execute the smart contract. Gas, therefore, acts as a barrier precluding complex or several contracts from overwhelming the EVM.

Because of these functional limitations, smart contracts today are best suited for simple tasks that are components of larger agreements. For example, smart contracts can ensure the automatic payment of funds upon certain triggering events.[103] They can also be used to impose financial penalties if certain objective conditions are not satisfied.[104] In both cases, human intervention is unnecessary once the contract deploys and is operational. This can reduce the execution and enforcement costs of the contracting process.[105]

4. THE BENEFITS OF SMART CONTRACTS

Smart-contract advocates tout efficiency, transparency, and security as some of the main benefits of using smart contracts.[106]

a. Reduced Costs and Automation

Smart contracts present opportunities to reduce or eliminate transaction costs in the traditional contracting process. Smart contracts can automate workflow and trigger downstream actions without human involvement. This automation of tasks via computer protocols can save countless hours in business processes. This may also eliminate the reliance on third-party institutions, such as banks, to transfer funds to employees.[107]

---

101. LUIT HOLLANDER, *The Ethereum Virtual Machine– How does it Work?* medium.com, (Jan 29, 2019).
102. CRYPTOCOMPARE. *What is the "Gas" in Ethereum?* cryptocompare.com, (Jul. 30, 2015).
103. STUART D. LEVI & ALEX LIPTON, *An Introduction to Smart Contracts and their Potential and Inherent Limitations* at 1, The Harvard Law School Forum on Corporate Governance, corpgov.law.harvard.edu, (May 26, 2018).
104. *Id.*
105. *Id.*
106. SADIKU et al., *Smart Contracts: A Primer,* 5 JOURNAL OF SCIENTIFIC AND ENGINEERING RESEARCH 538, (2018).
107. *Id.*

- Example: Businesses such as insurance companies, real-estate firms, and law firms can automate the release of money held in escrow upon the completion of terms set forth in an agreement.[108]
- Example: Employees can record their time or completed tasks onto a blockchain, which then triggers smart-contract conditions that issue payment to the employee.
- Example: Smart contracts can implement restrictive covenants that impose penalties or revoke access to resources if certain terms do not occur, or if certain conditions do occur.[109]

b. No Physical Documents Needed

Smart contracts reduce physical documentation. Because the program executes automatically once the condition set forth in the parameter occurs, there is no need to generate or file documents verifying that performance has occurred. The blockchain directly records the performance. Furthermore, the automation and secure digitization of documents can streamline processes across multiple parties, such as supply chains. Often, the efficiency of supply chains is reduced by paper-based systems that rely on the parties, and third parties like banks, physically transferring documents.[110] Signatures from multiple individuals appear on letters of credit, bills of lading, and other documents along the supply chain. Because digital documents often lack the security of physical documents, current IT systems at banks track the logistics of physical documents for trade finance.[111]

- Example: By incorporating digital documents onto the blockchain, secure, digital versions of key documents are available to all parties in a transaction. A smart contract can also be used to manage the workflow and trigger each step in the sequence as the preceding step completes.[112]

c. Reduced Reliance on Third Parties

The use of smart contracts can also reduce, or even eliminate, intermediaries in several industries. One application is the automatic

108. PHILLIP BAUKNIGHT & BROOKE YEGAN, *6 Reasons Why Employers Need to Join the Blockchain Revolution and Consider Smart Contracts*, jdsupra.com, (Jul. 14, 2021).
109. *Id.*
110. DAVID SCHATSKY, *Getting Smart About Smart Contracts*, Deloitte.com (2018), available at https://www2.deloitte.com/us/en/pages/finance/articles/cfo-insights-getting-smart-contracts.html.
111. *Id.*
112. *Id.*

dispensing of funds. Businesses such as banks, law firms, real-estate firms, and insurance companies, rely on third parties to hold funds in escrow. By using smart contracts, these businesses can trust that payment hinges on verifiable performance by the other party, and therefore they need not rely on an intermediary to handle the disbursement of funds. Smart contracts remove middlemen in many contexts, allowing businesses to reduce the cost of their operations.

- Example: By implementing a will into a smart contract bolstered by a blockchain network, the terms of the will ipso jure execute without needing an executor.[113]
- Example: In 2015, English singer-songwriter Imogen Heap developed the blockchain-based platform Mycelia. Mycelia aims to be a decentralized musical database for artists to share music.[114] Smart contracts encoded into the network allow fans to pay artists directly without involving record companies. Similarly, a blockchain-based e-reader would allow authors to upload their work directly to the blockchain, where customers could purchase the works directly from the authors via smart contracts.[115]

d. Transparency and Reduced Misunderstandings

Transparency is another key feature and benefit of smart contracts. Both the input parameters and execution steps need to be specific and objective. Clarity reduces the possibility of misunderstandings or mistakes when performing the agreement.

- Example: Since smart contracts must be reduced to computer code, there is little ambiguity over the terms of the agreement because of the specificity and detail required.

e. Traceability

Smart-contract agreements exist across a distributed, decentralized blockchain network. Therefore, the parties can track every step of the transaction. The entire performance of a contract becomes easily traceable over time by any involved party with the requisite permissions. If an item gets lost during the process, the smart contract can record when and how the disruption occurred.

113. LLOYD MARINO, *Blockchain – The end of the Middleman*, medium.com, (June 13, 2016).
114. IMOGEN HEAP & MATT GILES, *Imogen Heap & Hacking the Music Industry*, POPULAR SCIENCE at 44–45, Bonnier Corporation, (2016).
115. LLOYD MARINO, *Blockchain – The end of the Middleman*, medium.com, (June 13, 2016).

- Example: In the context of a supply chain, each party can instantly discern whether another party in the chain has performed its obligations, when the performance occurred, and what input parameter triggered the last step.

f. Immutability

The key characteristic of a smart contract, and likely the most attractive feature, is that no one can manipulate its contents or prevent its execution. Smart contracts are as secure as the blockchain network on which they are based. Cryptography secures the records on a blockchain.[116] Each participant in the network has a private key assigned to their transactions that acts as an individual digital signature.[117] The blockchain is decentralized and distributed across a peer-to-peer network. This network continuously updates and synchronizes. A massive amount of computing power, or at least 51% of the network, would have to alter the entire blockchain at once.[118] The larger the network, the less vulnerable it is to manipulation.

- Example: A smart contract is transferred to the blockchain. Once the triggering event occurs, the parties to the contract will be unable to prevent its execution.
- Example: If a participant attempts to alter a record, the signature becomes invalid, and the network receives a notification about the attempt.

g. Reduced Manipulation Potential

Public blockchains rely on agreement across the network to verify that a transaction occurs. The network participants must agree on the "truth" of each transaction recorded on the blockchain for the transaction to process. Although businesses may rely on public blockchain networks, many will prefer to use private blockchain networks to maintain confidentiality of information and to control the location of proprietary data. A private blockchain works like any other, except that only permitted parties may participate in the network. These are known as "permissioned smart contracts" and "permissioned blockchains."[119] Smaller than other networks, these private blockchains do not enjoy the

116. CURTIS MILES, *Blockchain security: What keeps your transaction data safe?* IBM Supply Chain and Blockchain Blog, (Dec. 12, 2017).
117. *Id.*
118. *Id.*
119. YINING HU et al., *Blockchain-Based Smart Contracts – Applications and Challenges,* (Jun. 11, 2019), available at https://arxiv.org/pdf/1810.04699.pdf

same inherent resistance to tampering as public blockchain networks. Private blockchains rely on a process called "selective endorsement," where identified users verify transactions to achieve consensus.[120] The advantage is that only participants with the appropriate authorization may access or maintain the transaction ledger. The security of the blockchain vests in the hands of just a few identified users and remains somewhat vulnerable to manipulation from the inside.

- Example: A company that uses a private blockchain is protected against resistance and manipulation, but not to the same degree as a public blockchain. That said, the company can implement integrated security infrastructure to reduce the risk of manipulation from within the network.[121]

h. Authentic Verification and Tamper-Proof System

By using distributed blockchain ledgers and other distributed ledger technologies, smart contracts maintain a verifiable and immutable record of all contract activity. Because the blockchain encodes the terms of the agreement (the input protocols and execution steps), they enjoy the same level of protection from manipulation. Finally, the automatic nature of the smart contract means that once a party performs its obligation and enters the correct input, the output is guaranteed to occur.

- Example: If the network is secure, the verified record of the smart contract is effectively immune from tampering or accidental errors.

5. CHALLENGES AND DISADVANTAGES OF SMART-CONTRACT USE

The adoption and implementation of smart contracts in the business world also has its challenges. The primary difficulties include using programmers and "off-chain" resources.

a. Reliance on Technical Experts

One key difficulty is that parties must rely on technical experts to either reduce the terms of a business arrangement into code or to verify that a third party's code accurately reflects the agreement.[122] Any non-programmer will be unable to discern even the most basic of smart

120. CURTIS MILES, *Blockchain security: What keeps your transaction data safe?* IBM Supply Chain and Blockchain Blog, (Dec. 12, 2017).

121. *Id.*

122. STUART D. LEVI & ALEX LIPTON, *An Introduction to Smart Contracts and their Potential and Inherent Limitations* at 4, The Harvard Law School Forum on Corporate Governance, corpgov.law.harvard.edu, (May 26, 2018).

contracts once reduced to their effective form. Although this is similar to how a lawyer must explain the legal effect of an agreement, it is more analogous to needing a translator for a document written in a foreign language.

- Example: A non-lawyer or a sophisticated businessperson can understand the basic terms of an agreement and even some of the more complicated provisions. Smart contracts, however, will be unintelligible to a reader who does not understand the contract's written code.

b. Limited Availability of Text Templates

Text templates can minimize the use of technical experts.[123] A text template is a set of pre-written instructions or parameters that the parties adopt and insert into the smart contract's program. But the availability of text templates is limited. Technical experts might need to create new templates, and all parties may need to hire lawyers who can draft the ancillary agreements and help the programmer discern the practical legal effects of the primary parties' contract. This process may create more transaction costs for the parties than it will save.

- Example: A simple smart contract deducts a late fee from a party's wallet if delivery fails to occur by a specific date. The text template provides a field for the penalty amount, the date of delivery, and the party that receives the penalty. These terms are then incorporated into the code of the smart contract without more input from the parties. But if an existing template is unavailable for this transaction, a new program (or a new template) must be created with help from technical experts. As a result, the transaction may require additional, ancillary agreements between one or more of the parties and the programmer that will develop the smart contract.

c. The Need for "Off-Chain" Resources

Many proposed use cases for smart contracts require the use of resources, inputs, or information off the blockchain. These are known as "off-chain" resources. Parties use an "oracle" to retrieve information that is off the chain and to push the information to the blockchain at predetermined times.[124] An oracle is a trusted third party or mechanism that supplies the information that the smart contract needs before it executes.

---

123. *Id.*
124. *Id.*

- Example: A smart contract is programmed to execute a transfer if the Los Angeles Rams win the Superbowl. The Superbowl occurs in the real world. It is not on the blockchain, and no one can determine the winner by referencing verified transactions. A source of information "off the chain" must provide the necessary details. Here, an individual person inputs the name of the winning team after the game. If the parties are savvy and favor automation, they can use artificial intelligence to scan internet search results and determine the winner based on publicly available information. Once the requisite information transfers to the blockchain, the smart contract will execute.
- Example: A pragmatic use case that reveals the need for off-chain resources is in the provision of utilities. Smart contracts are incorporated into water and electricity services so that consumers receive their charges based on how much they use the service. The oracle in this example is the water or electricity meter that measures the consumer's use. The meter links to the network on which the smart contract resides and updates the information about the consumer's use onto the blockchain. The smart contract uses this data to calculate the consumer's bills based on the rates written into the code of the smart contract and then transfers funds from the consumer to the utility company.

d. The Need to Ensure the Security and Trustworthiness of Oracles

Although oracles are a simple and effective solution to the problem posed by off-chain resources, they come with disadvantages as well. The oracle must be secure and trustworthy, or the contract will not function as intended. An oracle could become compromised and provide data that helps one of the parties, or it could fail to provide accurate data. Other issues may arise when a third party is providing the oracle service. The contracting parties will require separate agreements with the oracle, and the oracle could go out of business before the agreement completes. These complications make it harder for parties to use off-chain resources. And the more off-chain resources needed, the higher the transaction cost and the more risk to the integrity of the smart contract.

- Example: In the utility company example, an underhanded customer could hack into the meter and manipulate the information pushed to the blockchain.
- Example: In late 2020, Value DeFi, a yield farming and decentralized finance protocol, suffered an attack after an

unknown actor exploited a vulnerability in its centralized price oracle. DeFi (decentralized finance) protocols such as Value DeFi aim to recreate traditional financial systems, such as banks and exchanges, using blockchain technology and self-executing smart contracts. Someone or something had tricked the price oracle, which monitored the prices of various digital tokens, into undervaluing the tokens, leading to a loss of around six million dollars.[125]

e. Difficult to Amend or Revise

Another profound obstacle for smart contracts is that it can be difficult to adjudicate disputes, perhaps even more so than disputes that arise from traditional contracts. Smart contract advocates often contend that the automatic and objective nature of smart contracts will eliminate judicial dispute resolution because the parties bind themselves to whatever result the smart contract produces. It is true that smart contracts work well when both sides perform their obligations in the manner that the program expects. In those circumstances, the parties will probably not disagree with the smart contract's result. But even when both parties are doing their utmost to perform, errors in the code may cause unexpected, and undesired, results in execution.

- Example: Parties to an agreement that relies on a smart contract must determine how to allocate the risk of such technical malfunctions. In some cases, they may even seek to hold the developer or their technical experts liable for damages that flow from a technical failure. The developer, in turn, may contend that the parties were unclear about their expectations for the program. The resulting ambiguity makes litigation more likely and reduces the appeal of smart contracts compared to traditional agreements.

f. Inability to Account for Payment Disputes

An often touted benefit of smart contracts is that they can automate payment without using invoices or collection notices, and without obtaining a judgment from a court. Yet parties, especially sophisticated businesses, are constantly moving funds around. They do not usually maintain a single account, or blockchain-connected wallet, that has enough funds to cover every component of a long-term contract. Ultimately, smart contracts cannot eliminate the possibility of a payment dispute when a party fails to make the funds available.

---

125. ROBERT STEVENS, *After $6 Million Hack, Value Defi Turns to Chainlink for Help*, decrypt.co, (Nov. 19, 2020).

- Example: If a party that owes a sum of money under a smart contract fails to fund the wallet linked to the contract on a timely basis, the smart contract may fail to execute when it calculates that the requisite funds are unavailable. Although the parties may introduce multiple layers, such as backup wallets that the smart contract will seek to draw from in the event of an inadequately funded primary wallet, secondary sources may also fail to have requisite funds available.

g. Cannot Make Subjective Decisions or Judgments

It can be even harder to resolve a dispute when a party tries to perform but the counterparty believes the performance was inadequate. Issues that steer toward legal disputes involve subjective circumstances. Assume that the agreement between the parties links to a smart contract. For a smart contract to execute, the parameters must be specific and objective. One issue is that this determination relies on several off-chain resources. Smart contracts are not well-suited for contracts that involve subjective circumstances or ambiguities. Under these circumstances, the parties save time and money by not incorporating a smart contract into their agreement.

- Example: Consider a homeowner that hires a builder to install a new deck. The homeowner asks the builder to use a particular type of oak to build the deck. The contract states that the builder may, after exercising commercially reasonable efforts to acquire the oak, use a different type of comparable wood. After shopping around, the builder finds that the requested oak is expensive because of an unexpected shortage. Although the wood is technically available, the builder would earn little to no profit on the contract if he were to use it instead of an alternative. The builder decides to use a wood cheaper but comparable in quality. After discovering that the builder has used an alternative wood, the homeowner sues the builder, arguing that he failed to exercise commercially reasonable efforts to acquire the preferred wood. Yet the smart contract cannot determine the parties' satisfaction or whether breach has occurred. What was the market for lumber when the builder was purchasing materials? What efforts did the builder take to pinpoint the preferred type of wood? Another issue is the subjective and uncertain meaning of commercial reasonability. Should the builder have spent more time looking for a cheaper supply of the preferred wood? Is the builder's profit margin relevant to the commercial reasonability of using the alternative wood, or does the mere fact that the wood was available mean that the builder had to use it? In some cases, parties may be able to anticipate these ambiguities and build them into the smart contract. A clause may state, for example, that the builder is only obligated to purchase materials that cost up to 80% of the price of the contract (leaving some room for the cost of labor and profit). Yet the more eventualities built into the contract, the more complicated it becomes and the greater the transaction costs.

h. Inflexibility and Limited Application

The automatic and inflexible nature of smart contracts can limit their application. Once the parties negotiate, draft, and incorporate the smart contract onto a blockchain platform, it is hard to alter the program.

Depending on the circumstances, a party may feel that some performance is better than nothing. Commerce often benefits from this flexibility and willingness to adjust the precise terms of performance. Parties may be able to anticipate the circumstances that require flexibility and incorporate these terms into the agreement. But with more contingencies written into the agreement come more expenses, such as costs to draft, negotiate, and incorporate the agreement onto the blockchain. The objectivity of smart contracts may be too inflexible for the realities of how many business partners interact.

- Example: During a business relationship, parties may wish to overlook minor breaches and traditionally can do so by not enforcing the penalty provisions available. A supplier who values the business of a customer may wish to overlook a late payment to preserve the business relationship. But if this relationship is governed only by a smart contract, the vendor cannot overlook a late payment, and it will likely result in the automatic extraction of a late fee from the customer's wallet.

- Example: A party may be inclined to accept partial performance of a service, or even consider it full performance, to preserve a relationship. If the contract is for software services, it could result in the automatic suspension of the customer's access to a software program.

i. Inflexibility of Contract Modification or Adjustment

There are limitations to how a smart contract amends or terminates. Once implemented onto the blockchain, there is no easy way for the parties to adjust the terms of the agreement. With traditional contracts, parties can draft an amendment to alter the terms of an existing agreement. The amendment is incorporated (more or less) seamlessly into the existing terms of the contract. But with a blockchain-based smart contract, the characteristics that define the smart contract also hamper the parties' ability to adjust it. Again, technological developments will likely make it easier for parties to adjust the terms of their smart contracts. But the high cost of amendment limits the widespread acceptance of smart contracts.

- Example: Once written onto the blockchain, the smart contract is both immutable and automatic. Modifying the code of a smart contract is harder than modifying standard software code that is not on the blockchain.

j. Inflexibility of Contract Termination

The termination of smart contracts is also limited. The automatic and immutable nature of the agreement will make it costly to terminate or amend the smart contract's program. The inflexible nature of smart contracts means that many types of dynamic business practices are not always translatable into the code of the program.

- Example: After negotiating an agreement and encoding the smart contract onto the blockchain, one of the parties realizes that an error in the agreement gives the other party some right that the parties did not intend to transfer. The parties could have easily amended this error with traditional contracting.
- Example: A party may realize during an agreement that it is more cost-effective for the party not to fulfil its obligations. Consider a simple contract for the sale of goods. The seller may receive an offer from a third party who wishes to purchase the goods for five times the price agreed to by the original purchaser. The enhanced value from the higher sale price might outweigh the damages that the seller will incur from breaching the original purchase agreement. This is impossible with smart contracts.
- Example: Ceasing performance, even temporarily, may lead to negotiation for better terms. This too is impossible with smart contracts.

k. Software and Security Issues

Despite the inherent security features of blockchain technology, security remains one of the most significant hurdles for the widespread adoption of smart contracts. At their core, smart contracts are based in software. Therefore, they are prone to security issues. Blockchain platforms host smart contracts. These platforms have their own languages for developers to write smart contract programs. The Ethereum network, for example, allows developers to run programs written in Solidity, a programming language intended for writing smart contracts.[126] It was first proposed in 2014 and later developed by Ethereum's Solidity team.[127] Thousands of developers use it to create blockchain-based services and programs. While smart contracts can be easy to write with Solidity, it is also difficult to write them securely. Other, more common programming languages may also be used to write smart contracts. But no matter what language one writes the program in, bugs and vulnerabilities in the source code can create security issues for the smart contracts.[128]

- Example: In October 2021, a popular DeFi platform called Compound mistakenly transferred $90 million worth of its native cryptocurrency tokens, known as COMP tokens, to users because of faulty coding.[129] The issue arose after Compound rolled out a standard system upgrade. Soon after implementation, someone discovered erroneously large transfers and that a bug in one of the system's core smart contracts was the culprit. Even worse, because any changes to the protocol required a seven-day governance process, no one could implement the fix for over a week.[130]

There have also been cases of hackers intentionally exploiting errors in smart-contract coding to drain users' accounts. According to a report released in August 2021 by the blockchain-analytics company CipherTrace, DeFi hacks led to about $361 million in losses between January and July 2021.[131] All crypto-related thefts, hacks, and frauds totaled $681 million over the same period.[132]

- Example: In August 2021, hackers exploited a vulnerability in the DeFi platform Poly Network and stole tokens worth more than $600 million.[133] Poly Network facilitates peer-to-peer transactions

---

126. CALVIN EBUN-AMU, *What is Solidity and How is it used to Develop Smart Contracts?* makeuseof.com, (Apr. 19, 2021).
127. *Id.*
128. MARCELL GOGAN, *Smart Contract Security: What are the Weak Spots of Ethereum, Eos, and Neo Networks?* technative.io, (Dec. 13, 2018).
129. MACKENZIE SIGALOS, *Defi Bug Accidentally Gives $90 Million to Users, Founder Begs Them to Return It*, cnbc.com, (Oct. 1, 2021).
130. *Id.*
131. CIPHERTRACE. *Cryptocurrency Crime and Anti-Money Laundering Report, August 2021.* ciphertrace.com (2021), available at https://ciphertrace.com/cryptocurrency-crime-and-anti-money-laundering-report-august-2021/
132. *Id.*
133. GERTRUDE CHAVEZ-DREYFUSS & MICHELLE PRICE, *Explainer: How Hackers Stole and Returned $600 Mln in Tokens from Poly Network*, reuters.com, (Aug. 12, 2021).

with a focus on allowing users to move tokens between various blockchains.[134] Users could, for example, transfer Bitcoin from the Ethereum Blockchain to the Binance Smart Chain, another popular blockchain platform. Poly Network uses a smart contract to transfer tokens between the blockchains. To do so, the platform must maintain a large amount of liquidity that allows users to swap tokens. The hackers managed to override the smart-contract instructions and divert funds to three wallets.[135] Ultimately, the hackers returned all the diverted tokens. They claimed that the hack was a stunt designed to expose the platform's vulnerability, but others have suggested they got cold feet after encountering difficulty laundering the tokens. This incident exposes the serious risks that overreliance on smart contracts can create.

6. USE CASES FOR SMART CONTRACTS

In some industries, smart contracts are already used to supplement, or even replace, traditional contracts. But the development of smart contracts is still in the preliminary stages. Many of the smart contracts used today are limited to transferring funds upon certain triggering events or imposing penalties if certain conditions fail to occur. Even in their limited condition, smart contracts are already used to carry out thousands to millions of transactions. In January 2020, there were over one million smart contracts deployed on the Ethereum network alone.[136] This was a hundredfold increase over the preceding two years.[137] Despite the difficulties discussed in the previous section, some theorize that smart contracts will dominate nearly all forms of commerce. Whether smart contracts remain limited to their current use cases or become as commonplace as credit cards, there is no question that they are here to stay and that the contracting landscape will continue to be impacted by their development.

a. Banking and Finance

The banking and finance industries are very susceptible to using smart contracts. The blockchain provides a single ledger as the source of truth, and smart contracts can automate approval workflows and clearing calculations prone to lag and error. The automation of these processes can reduce the likelihood of errors, lower costs, and reduce

134. *Id.*

135. *Id.*

136. JAMES BARTON, *How Many Ethereum Smart Contracts Are There?* coindiligent.com, (Jan. 27, 2020).

137. *Id.*

the time to settlement.[138] Trade clearing and settlement entail labor-intensive activities, requiring approvals and complicated internal and external reconciliations. Independent processing by counterparties causes discrepancies, which lead to costly resolutions and settlement delays.[139] These processes limit trade finance systems and result in higher risk and costs. Blockchain and smart contracts could streamline these processes.

- Example: When a bank offers a loan or trade funding to a customer, the bank must verify the customer's identity to comply with KYC and AML requirements. Obtaining a customer's information, like their credit history, from other institutions can be difficult and costly.[140] Smart contracts can automate processes related to KYC and AML that consume significant time and resources by verifying information based on blockchain records.[141] Counterparties could learn salient information about individuals or entities without knowing their identity.

- Example: IBM is working with multiple banks and financial institutions to implement a digital trade chain based in blockchain technology that can enhance efficiency, transparency, and security.[142]

DeFi platforms, which present an alternative to traditional financial services, rely on smart contracts. Many DeFi protocols provide parallel services to the banking and financial services industry, such as lending, borrowing, and trading. Users can participate in this new form of financial service without the centralized custody of funds or fees by intermediaries.[143] Rather than use a neutral third party, DeFi uses an application through blockchain technology, also known as a DeFi protocol, to directly link users.[144] Although the DeFi sector is only a few years old, DeFi projects have already captured billions of dollars in value, and this trend of growth is set to continue in the near term.

---

138. JOHN REAM, YAN CHU, & DAVID SCHATSKY, *Upgrading Blockchains,* deloitte.com, (Jun. 8, 2016).
139. *Id.*
140. MAHIPAL NEHRA, *What's The Role of Smart Contracts in The Banking Industry?* readwrite.com, (Aug. 26, 2021).
141. IVAN KOT, *Smart Contract Applications, Limitations and Future Outlook,* itransition.com, (Jan. 28, 2021).
142. IBM MEDIA CENTER. "Banks team with IBM for Blockchain Powered Trade Finance," [Video], available at https://mediacenter.ibm.com/media/1_kw5fky0r
143. CRYPTOPEDIA, *Real World Examples of Smart Contracts*, gemini.com, (Dec. 23, 2021).
144. NICOLE SANDERS, *What is DEFI and How Does It Work?* taxbit.com, (Sep. 29, 2021).

b. Insurance

Some insurance contracts are more efficient when made with smart contracts. Disaster insurance, for example, is well-suited to the incorporation of smart contracts. When the event is easily verifiable and describable through measurable data, such as in the context of weather-index insurance, smart contracts could enhance the efficiency of claims processing.

- Example: A farmer and an insurance company agree to encode the terms of a weather index insurance policy into a smart contract. The smart contract connects to an oracle that pushes weather data onto the blockchain. Depending on the value of the rainfall index, the smart contract either executes and issues a claim to the farmer or expires.

This is an example of parametric insurance, which uses triggers or indexes rather than submitted claims to issue a payment after an event has occurred. To date, the adoption of parametric insurance has been limited because there was a lack of the necessary infrastructure to execute payments and collect data in a rapid and secure manner.[145]

With recent advances in blockchain technology, parametric insurance policies grounded in smart contracts can refine the efficiency of insurance services. In the case of the weather index policy, individuals could write the smart contract to interact with the internal system of the financial institution to verify the payment of premiums and extract claim payments.[146] Automating these processes can boost efficiency and streamline the claim verification process, thus reducing costs for both parties.

- Example: The motor insurance industry can flourish with added efficiency through smart contracts.[147] Today, car insurance involves several complex and cost-intensive processes. Under most insurance policies, the insurer will reimburse the customer for damages that the customer was not responsible for, such as certain collisions or mechanical failures. In the event of damage to

145. SIBYLLE FISCHER, *Smart Contracts and the Future of Insurance*, baloise.com, (Jul. 28, 2021).
146. THE WORLD BANK GROUP, *Smart Contract Technology and Financial Inclusion*, (2020), available at https://openknowledge.worldbank.org/bitstream/handle/10986/33723/Smart-Contract-Technology-and-Financial-Inclusion.pdf?sequence=5&isAllowed=y
147. LENNART BADER et al., *Smart Contract-Based Car Insurance Policies*, (Dec, 2018), available at https://www.researchgate.net/profile/Roman-Matzutt/publication/327987487_Smart_Contract- Based_Car_Insurance_Policies/links/5d243c60299bf1547ca4fc87/Smart-Contract-Based-Car-Insurance-Policies.pdf

the vehicle, the customer must submit a claim for reimbursement. The insurer must then determine whether they should reimburse the customer under the policy.

The availability of reliable data is crucial for the insurer to determine whether a claim is reimbursable. The recent emergence of tamper-resistant sensors and electronic control units provides a feasible solution so that insurers can acquire accurate data about a collision with a lower possibility of manipulation by the customer.[148] In clear cases in which the data reveals that the insurer should reimburse a claim, there is no need for a surveyor to manually inspect the vehicle or investigate the incident. Eliminating the use of a surveyor reduces costs and streamlines the claim process for both parties. Smart contracts, informed by tamper-resistant sensors, may provide the foundation for defining the conditions under which claims should reimburse.

c. Supply-Chain Management

As the economies of the world have become intertwined, global commerce has come to rely on global supply chains. Even the simplest of consumer goods may require the input of thousands of different people from a dozen countries. In a 1980 PBS television show, Milton Friedman famously used the story "I, Pencil" by Leonard Read (written in 1958) to illustrate the complex process needed to produce something as simple as a pencil. The chain of production delineated by Friedman over forty years ago has only become more complex.

Today, supply chains involve stakeholders and business transactions. They are complex and face challenges, such as the lack of transparency and traceability, the difficulty of managing disruptions, and the requirement of trust between contracting parties. Smart contracts can reduce complexity in a supply chain through automated verification and execution of multiple business transactions.[149] They can be used to determine the provenance of goods, track the chain of custody as goods flow through the supply chain, execute payment upon the fulfilment of necessary criteria, and provide a database of stakeholders. Furthermore, a decentralized, immutable, and transparent record provides all stakeholders with access to necessary information and helps build trust among them.

- Example: Since 2018, the U.S. home-improvement store Home Depot has been tracking purchases from some of its suppliers

148. *Id.*
149. ANGWEI LAW. *Smart Contracts and their Application in Supply Chain Management,* Thesis: S.M. in Engineering and Management, Massachusetts Institute of Technology, System Design and Management Program, (2017), available at https://dspace.mit.edu/handle/1721.1/114082

with blockchain technology.[150] Disputes can easily arise between purchasers and suppliers as to the quality or quantity of shipped goods. By using a distributed ledger, fewer disputes arise because both sides can see the flow of product from one party to the next in real time. This also allows both parties to quickly identify where a problem occurs in the supply chain and to allocate responsibility accordingly.

d. Real Estate

Smart contracts and blockchain technology will likely become a fundamental component of real-estate record keeping and transactions. Brokers, lawyers, banks, and escrow services have played defining roles in the real-estate industry for a long time. Blockchain and smart contracts could modify or remove the need for these roles. The mortgage loan process relies on a complex system to provide the origination, funding, and servicing of mortgages.[151] Smart contracts could reduce the costs of this process through automation, redesign, and shared access to secure electronic versions of physical legal documents.[152] Costs could be reduced even further by involving external partners, such as credit scoring companies, land registry offices, and tax authorities in the blockchain-based process, thereby facilitating faster processing.[153]

- Example: An area for potential refinement is multiple-listing services, or *MLS*. Participants in the real-estate market use MLS platforms to access property-level data. Because of the lack of standardized processes and substantive human intervention, information is often inaccurate, out-of-date, or incomplete.[154] A blockchain-based MLS could distribute data across a peer-to-peer network in a manner that allows brokers to govern the data more effectively and enhances trust in listings. This blockchain-based MLS could provide coherent and accurate property data, giving

---

150. NICK DUNBAR, *Home Depot's Treasury Puts Suppliers on Blockchain – EuroFinance: The Global Treasury Community*, eurofinance.com, (Sep. 20, 2018).
151. BART CANT et al., *Smart Contracts in Financial Services: Getting From Hype to Reality* at 10, capgemini.com, (2016), available at https://www.capgemini.com/consulting-de/wp-content/uploads/sites/32/2017/08/smart_contracts_paper_long_0.pdf
152. *Id.*
153. *Id.* at 11.
154. SURABHI KEJRIWAL & SURAUBH MAHAJAN, *Blockchain in Commercial Real Estate*, deloitte.com, (2020), available at https://www2.deloitte.com/us/en/pages/financial-services/articles/blockchain-in-commercial-real-estate.html

market participants access to more reliable data at a lower cost.[155] The tech-focused real-estate company REX has already begun testing the technology for a blockchain-based MLS service.[156]

The current system of paper-based property titles imposes significant transaction costs upon the real-estate market. There may be issues with the authenticity of mortgage and title documents, or the accuracy of any liens or other information attached to the title.[157] Parties must purchase title insurance, increasing the cost of their transaction, and title disputes may impact a buyer's ownership of a property. Some estimates suggest that people spend nearly $1 billion annually on title-fraud resolutions.[158] A system of land recording based on blockchain technology could mitigate many issues inherent to the paper-based recording system. The distributed and tamper-proof nature of the blockchain makes it hard for bad actors to engage in fraud related to liens, easements, or other matters. The risk of title fraud and the cost of title checks could be reduced through a blockchain-based system. Smart contracts can replace escrow services by holding funds in trust and distributing the funds upon performance of the agreement.

- Example: Some national governments have implemented plans to use blockchain platforms for land-title registries. Georgia, Ukraine, Brazil, Honduras, and the United Arab Emirates have all begun to refine their land registry and transfer processes with the use of blockchain and smart-contract technology.[159]

- Example: The advent of fractional ownership also presents an opportunity for innovation and disruption of the industry. Traditionally, investments in real estate require a lot of capital and a substantial time investment. Fractional ownership and tokenization allow investors to buy or sell fractions of a piece of real estate. On the flip side, a property owner can leverage their property by putting fractions of their real estate onto the market to get quick access to cash while still enjoying the use of the property.

155. *Id.*
156. *Id.*
157. *Id.*
158. *Id.*
159. QIUYUN SHANG & ALLISON PRICE, *A Blockchain-Based Land Titling Project in the Republic of Georgia: Rebuilding Public Trust and Lessons for Future Pilot Projects*, 12 INNOVATIONS: TECHNOLOGY, GOVERNANCE, GLOBALIZATION 3–4 at 72, (Jan. 1, 2019).

e. Broader Use Cases

Organizations in any industry must keep financial records in one form or another. Smart contracts may keep these records and provide an accurate and transparent means for companies to collect and record data.

By implementing smart contracts to collect data, it is easier for companies to uniformly collect information across the organization, thereby reducing the costs of audits and accounting. It also facilitates financial data exchanges between business partners and improve the trustworthiness of the parties' information.

- Example: One industry that stands to benefit from this process is healthcare. The computer systems for the world's healthcare industries hold hundreds of millions of patient medical records as well as other critical data and information. Blockchain technology allows entire databases of health records to be encrypted and stored securely while allowing individual patients easy access to their personal health records. Smart contracts also help manage patient care by issuing reminders for follow-up appointments or sending out regular prescriptions automatically.

7. THE LEGAL STATUS OF SMART CONTRACTS

a. Enforceability and Relationship to Traditional Contracts

A smart contract is not a legal agreement or contract in the traditional sense. Rather, it is a computer program that performs a task when triggered by the occurrence of a predetermined event. If the parties wish, a smart contract could constitute a legal agreement if it includes the necessary elements: (1) ***A Valid Offer,*** (2) ***An Acceptance, and*** (3) ***Consideration.***

For example, two parties could reach a verbal understanding of their business arrangement and then reduce that understanding into executable code.[160] The legal status and enforceability of these "code-only" smart contracts remain uncertain. As a result, parties that wish to use smart contracts to carry out the provisions of a commercial arrangement will rely on a traditional, text-based agreement that itself references the use of the smart contract to bring about the relevant provisions.

160. STUART D. LEVI & ALEX LIPTON, *An Introduction to Smart Contracts and their Potential and Inherent Limitations* at 2, The Harvard Law School Forum on Corporate Governance, corpgov.law.harvard.edu, (May 26, 2018).

The enforceability and interpretation of contracts in the United States depends on state law; there is no federal contract law in the United States.[161] State courts traditionally look to whether the parties satisfy the common law requirements of (1) offer, (2) acceptance, and (3) consideration. A traditional text-based contract that refers to a smart contract could meet these requirements. Most agreements do not have to be in writing to be enforceable.

- Example: Consider the vending machine again. When you put money into the machine and select an item, you are creating a contract, even though there are no written terms other than the price displayed. Within certain limitations (the statute of frauds, for example), the fact that individuals delineate an agreement only in code does not preclude contract formation.

There are other reasons that suggest that society is ready to introduce legally enforceable smart contracts. The Uniform Electronic Transactions Act (UETA), which dates to 1999 and provides the basis for state law in forty-seven states, provides that, with certain exceptions, electronic records (which includes records created by a computer program) should have the same legal effect as their written counterparts.[162] The Act recognizes the validity of "electronic agents," which it defines as a computer program or other automated means used independently to trigger an action or respond to electronic records or performances in whole or in part, without review or action by an individual.[163] That sounds a lot like a smart contract, which can respond to any number of actions or occurrences once activated—within the confines of its programming—and without human intervention.

Comparably, the federal Electronic Signatures Recording Act recognizes the validity of electronic signatures and electronic records in interstate commerce. [164] It also provides that contracts or records relating to a transaction may not be denied legal effect just because the formation, creation, or delivery involved the action of one or more electronic agents if electronic agent's action is legally attributable to the party.[165]

Although existing law does suggest that smart contracts may constitute legally enforceable agreements, there is still significant uncertainty.

161. *Id.*

162. *Id.* at 3.

163. Uniform Electronic Transactions Act § 2(6) (Unif. Law Comm'n 1999).

164. STUART D. LEVI & ALEX LIPTON, *An Introduction to Smart Contracts and their Potential and Inherent Limitations* at 3, The Harvard Law School Forum on Corporate Governance, corpgov.law.harvard.edu, (May 26, 2018).

165. *Id.*

Relying on laws that predate the development of blockchain technology, and the more widespread adoption of smart contracts cannot provide legal certainty and reassurance that businesses require. Fortunately, many U.S. states and other jurisdictions have begun to address smart contracts and provide a legal framework within which parties can use smart contracts with confidence.

b. How Some Jurisdictions Are Addressing Smart Contracts

There is little to no case law in the United States that directly addresses the enforceability of smart contracts. There has also been little to no action by the federal government to address the use of smart contracts. In 2018, the United States Congress did release a joint economic report that referenced blockchain technology and the use of smart contracts.[166] The report stated that although smart contracts "might sound new, the concept is rooted in basic contract law."[167] "With smart contracts, a program enforces the contract built into the code."[168]

Although these statements lack the force of law, the report tacitly recognizes that the code of a smart contract could contain or reflect the terms of a legally binding contract. Over the past few years, several states have passed smart-contract legislation with varying degrees of detail and success.[169] In general, these legislative initiatives fall into three broad categories: (1) ***The formation of exploratory committees,*** (2) ***The recognition of basic smart contract concepts, or*** (3) ***The comprehensive regulation of smart contracts and their related technologies.***

Forming Exploratory Committees

Exploratory task forces are usually the first step states take to research the potential applications of smart contracts or blockchain technology and determine the appropriate legislative approach. Sometimes committees are responsible for researching applications, such as the use of blockchain technology in elections.[170]

- Examples: California, New York, New Jersey, and Texas have all formed committees to explore smart contracts, blockchain technology, and their related applications.

166. JOINT ECONOMIC COMMITTEE CONGRESS OF THE UNITED STATES, *The 2018 Joint Economic Report* at 210, (2018).
167. *Id.*
168. *Id.*
169. CHRISTOPHER ADCOCK, *An Update on State Smart Contract Legislation*, 12 THE NATIONAL LAW REVIEW 188, (Apr. 15, 2020).
170. *Id.*

Recognizing Basic Smart-Contract Concepts

Some states have already passed or have pending legislation that establishes a basic framework for the use of smart contracts in state commerce. These statutes use a combination of approaches, such as adding certain definitions to business codes, recognizing the validity of smart contracts under the law, or permitting the use of the related technologies.[171]

- Examples: States such as Arkansas, Maryland, Nevada, New York, Oklahoma, South Dakota, Texas, Utah, and Washington have passed legislation on smart-contract concepts. Other states, such as Connecticut and New Jersey, have seen this kind of legislation fail to pass or languish in committees.

Regulating Smart Contracts and their Related Technologies

Some states have taken a more comprehensive approach and adopted legislation that addresses the use of smart contracts by creating protections and limitations on their use. The next examples unveil some of the successful efforts to implement legislation that governs the use of smart contracts and blockchain technology:

- **Arizona**: In 2017, Arizona amended the Arizona Electronic Transactions Act (AETA)—its state-law equivalent of the UETA—to clarify that electronic records, electronic signatures, and smart-contract terms secured through blockchain technology are an electronic signature under AETA.[172] The statute also provides that a contract relating to a transaction may not be denied legal effect, validity, or enforceability just because that contract has a "smart-contract term." The statute provides definitions for "blockchain technology" and "smart contracts" that give certainty to contracting parties (and courts) as to the general meaning of these terms. The state enacted this legislation to energize the development of blockchain technology. Around the same time, the state passed legislation to restrict the use of blockchain as a tool for electronic firearm-tracking technology.[173]

- **Nevada**: Nevada has also taken an active hand in encouraging the development of blockchain-based industries. Nevada passed legislation in 2017 that provided legal definitions for the terms

171. *Id.*

172. JEFFREY NEUBURGER, *Arizona Passes Groundbreaking Blockchain and Smart Contract Law – State Blockchain Laws on the Rise,* New Media and Technology Law Blog, newmedialaw.proskauer.com, (Apr. 20, 2017).

173. *Id.*

critical to the use of smart contracts and blockchain technology.[174] These include new definitions for the terms "blockchain" and "smart contract" as well as updated definitions for "electronic record" and "electronic signature" that encompass blockchain-based versions of these items. Nevada's legislation tries to invigorate the development of blockchain-based business by prohibiting local governments from taxing, licensing, and imposing other requirements on the use of blockchain technology.

- **California**: Like Arizona, California amended its Electronic Transactions Act in 2018 to include definitions for blockchain technology and smart contracts. The amendment clarified that the definition of "contract" includes a smart contract, which is defined as "an event-driven program that runs on a distributed, decentralized, shared, and replicated ledger that can take custody over, and instruct transfer of, assets on that ledger."[175] It also updated the definitions of electronic record and electronic signature to include records or signatures secured through blockchain technology.
- **Tennessee**: Also in 2018, Tennessee enacted legislation that recognizes blockchain signatures and smart contracts as legally binding.[176] The bill, passed unanimously by the Tennessee General Assembly, acknowledges signatures secured through blockchain as electronic signatures, and records or contracts secured through blockchain as electronic records. It also provides definitions for "blockchain technologies" and "smart contracts," and states that a contract cannot be denied legal effect just because that contract includes a smart-contract term.
- **Iowa**: The Iowa legislature has introduced multiple pieces of legislation that would facilitate the use of blockchain technology and smart contracts for electronic transactions. The bills contain definitions for terms like "virtual currency," "distributed ledger technology," "smart contract," and "electronic signature" to clarify and establish the legal status of these items. Both the Iowa House

174. LUKE PARKER, *Nevada Protects Blockchains and Smart Contracts from Government Taxes, Licenses, and Certifications,* bravenewcoin.com, (Jun. 7, 2017).
175. PAUL HOW, *California Passes Bill Recognizing Smart Contracts, Blockchain Tech*, coingeek.com, (Aug. 31, 2018).
176. MARK SATTER, *Blockchain, Smart Contracts Now Legally Binding in Tennessee,* statescoop.com, (Mar. 26, 2018).

of Representatives and Senate passed their pieces of proposed legislation in early 2021.[177]

- **Wyoming**: Wyoming has perhaps become the most crypto-friendly jurisdiction in the United States. Although it is better known for mining (the traditional kind) and agriculture, the state has introduced some of the most comprehensive blockchain legislation in the world. Laws enacted in 2018 and 2019 clarified the treatment of digital assets in commercial law and set up a legal foundation for the use of smart contracts.[178] They also made it easier for crypto investors to set up limited-liability companies in Wyoming, enabling them to store their digital assets there for legal purposes while still living outside the state. Wyoming banks can serve as custodians of digital assets under a novel legal framework that permits institutional investors to retain ownership of digital assets through a custodian bank.[179] New legislation also required the Wyoming Division of Banking to issue a new type of banking charter to banks that deal mainly in digital assets. Kraken Bank, a subsidiary of the popular cryptocurrency exchange Kraken, became the first bank to be issued this charter in September 2020.[180]

A Special Note on Wyoming DAOs

In July 2021, Wyoming passed legislation that clarifies the legal status of decentralized autonomous organizations, or "DAOs."[181] DAOs are basically just software running on a blockchain platform. A set of rules govern DAOs. Individuals write these rules directly into code, and they are enforced by the blockchain network. The DAO stakeholders who come together to create the DAO decide on the initial rules. The stakeholders acquire a stake by investing capital in the DAO. This investment provides the investor with "governance tokens," a special form of cryptocurrency used to affect decision-making in the DAO.

Once the DAO is live, new participants may be able to purchase these tokens to earn the ability to participate in the DAO's governance. DAOs try to mimic a company structure where individuals build rules and regulations into the code and enforce them using smart contracts. Unlike in traditional organizations, DAOs do not have a defined hierarchy.

---

177. JAKE SLOBE, *Iowa House Approves Bill to Legally Recognize Blockchain Smart Contracts*, clayandmilk.com, (Apr. 2, 2021).
178. CHRIS MATTHEWS, *How Wyoming Became the Promised Land for Bitcoin Investors*, marketwatch.com, (Apr. 23, 2021).
179. *Id.*
180. *Id.*
181. MICHAEL DILL & HOLLAND & HART LLP, *Crypto, DAOs, and the Wyoming Frontier*, jdsupra.com, (Jul. 20, 2021).

Rather, the community of participants—who use the DAO's digital tokens to propose and vote on changes to the DAO's rules—make decisions based on a consensus. Recall the DeFi protocols discussed earlier in this chapter. Some form of DAO governs most major DeFi applications today. Under the new Wyoming law, DAOs have been granted the ability to use the LLC entity form if they meet other requirements, such as maintaining a registered agent for service of process.[182] The DAO's articles of organization may define it as either member managed or algorithmically managed.

SUMMARY

Smart contracts are impacting both sophisticated business transactions and simple consumer contracts. Yet smart contracts still lack widespread acceptance. New technological innovations can promulgate mainstream adoption faster than is expected. There appears to be a potential for unexpected technological disruption that will shift the paradigm in unforeseen ways. Most obstacles may be human rather than technological. Regulatory uncertainty and a lack of confidence in (or understanding of) the technology may impede the overall adoption of these new methodologies.

Smart contracts and blockchain technology can be considered an example of Amara's law in action. Amara's law, coined by Roy Amara—a researcher, scientist, and futurist who worked at the Stanford Research Institute—states that people tend to overestimate the effects of a technology in the short run and underestimate the effect. There is currently enormous interest in blockchain technology, and theories abound as to how it will change how our society functions. The soaring value of cryptocurrencies like Bitcoin and Ethereum fuels this interest. The astounding profits reaped by cryptocurrency speculators have captured the focus of governments, corporations, and individual investors around the world. But it is far more likely that the changes resulting from the wider acceptance of blockchain, and smart contracts will be slow, piecemeal, and undramatic. Blockchain and its applications may become a fundamental component in many industries such that one may have trouble remembering how society functioned without them.

For attorneys, especially attorneys that serve commercial clients, blockchain and smart contracts are an inevitable part of their future practice. What remains to be seen is not whether businesses will begin using smart contracts, but how far businesses will take them. It also remains to be seen just how smart contracts will impact the practice of law. It may become commonplace for lawyers to have programmer

182. *Id.*

expert witnesses testify on the meaning of certain code provisions. People may need programmers just as they use translators in court to interpret foreign languages. Transactional attorneys will use the services of developers to encode the terms of business agreements into smart contracts or to review a smart contract written by another party's developer. In the context of criminal law, blockchain can be used to verify the chain of custody for evidence (both physical and digital). For IP lawyers, blockchain can provide evidence of creation, first use, and assist in rights management. It can track distribution of material and help prevent copyright infringement. Smart contracts allow authors and artists to set up terms of sale and licensing for their intellectual property. The self-executing licenses, based in smart contracts, also ensure that the artist gets paid for the use of their work.

No matter what your practice area, it will benefit you to stay up to date with new developments involving smart contracts. Before you know it, smart contracts may be as commonplace and unremarkable as their vending-machine ancestors.

§ 9 Transactional Law

Bitcoin's rapid price increase in 2017 planted the seed for an unprecedented idea: using digital assets to raise capital. The result: an ICO boom occurred that same year. After a short recess, the ICO boom and crypto transactions are back and showing no signs of slowing down. But ICOs are less regulated than traditional investment vehicles—if regulated at all. Thus, these offerings bring an increased risk of legal action.

1. SPIKE IN CRYPTO TRANSACTIONS AND LAWSUITS

After 2017, digital-asset-related lawsuits, including those involving claims of unregistered ICOs, spiked. This can be traced to three events involving the SEC: (1) the DAO Report; (2) a cease-and-desist order to Munchee, Inc.; and (3) the SEC statement on cryptocurrencies and ICOs.

The DAO Report. In July 2017, the SEC released its investigative report on the Decentralized Autonomous Organization's (DAO) coin offering. The SEC concluded that the DAO tokens were investment contracts—or securities—under *Howey*, obligating the DAO to register the tokens with the SEC.[183] The DAO failed to register its tokens and did not qualify for a registration exemption. The DAO had engaged in an offering of unregistered securities. The SEC declined to bring an enforcement action and instead published an advisory opinion for future, similar cases. This DAO Report led to more awareness of ICOs and served as an acknowledgment—or, perhaps, a warning—to coin/token issuers that they must register their offerings, meet an applicable exemption, or risk liability under the *Howey* Test for engaging in an unregistered securities offering.

183. SEC Release No. 81207, DAO Report, (Jul. 25, 2017), available at https://www.sec.gov/litigation/investreport/34-81207.pdf

Munchee Cease-and-Desist. At the end of 2017, the SEC issued a cease-and-desist order to Munchee, Inc. in connection with its digital token offering. Munchee's ICO raised about $15 million by selling "MUN" tokens that would increase in value based on the company's efforts and allow individuals to trade the tokens on secondary markets. The cease-and-desist order underscored that the SEC will examine whether a digital asset is a "security" no matter how the issuer characterizes its ICO issuance. Ultimately, the SEC did not penalize Munchee because its investors had not suffered a loss.

Cryptocurrency/ICO Statement. In December 2017, SEC Chairman Jay Clayton released a statement on cryptocurrencies and ICOs, which clarified distinctions between digital assets that may be securities and assets that may not be securities. By issuing this statement, the SEC made clear its intention to monitor and enforce the securities laws on ICOs.

Private ICO litigation is unlike government action. For example, with private litigation involving whether a digital asset is a security, it is the judge or jury—not the SEC—who determines that issue under the *Howey* Test. A review of recent litigation shows how private parties are drafting their complaints and how judges and juries are treating digital-asset litigation.

Recall that each of the four *Howey* elements must be satisfied for the asset to be a security: (1) an investment of money, (2) in a common enterprise, (3) with an expectation of profits, and (4) derived solely from the efforts of others. In *SEC v. Shavers*, the district court applied the *Howey* Test and concluded that the Bitcoin Savings and Trust (BTCST) investment opportunities were "securities:"

> Bitcoin can be used as money. It can be used to purchase goods or services, and as Shavers stated, used to pay for individual living expenses. . . However, it can also be exchanged for conventional currencies, such as the U.S. dollar, Euro, Yen, and Yuan. Therefore, Bitcoin is a currency or form of money, and investors wishing to invest in BTCST provided an investment of money. . . [T]he investors here were dependent on Shaver's expertise in Bitcoin markets and his local connections. In addition, Shavers allegedly promised a substantial return on their investments as a result of his trading and exchanging Bitcoin. . . Clearly any investors participating in the BTCST investments were expecting profits from the efforts of Shavers.[184]

184. *SEC v. Shavers*, No. 4:13–CV–416, 2013 WL 4028182, at 3-4, (E.D. Tex. Aug. 6, 2013).

2. FROM IPO TO ICOS AND NOW STOS

Despite the popularity of coins and tokens, IPOs are still a significant part of capital formation. An IPO is the first time a company offers its stock to the public. To comply with the federal securities laws, individuals and companies must register public offerings with the SEC or meet an applicable exemption. If the company registers its offering with the SEC, it must file a registration statement using Form S-1. The registration statement must also include the prospectus—the offering document used to solicit investors. A prospectus contains critical company information, details on the directors, information on the shares offered and the class of shares, voting rights, minimum subscription amount, and other details to guide investors to make informed decisions. When reviewing the company's registration statement, the SEC focuses on whether it contains sufficient investor disclosures. If not, the company may have to revise its prospectus. Once the individual or company addresses all identified issues, the SEC declares the registration statement effective, and the company may proceed with its IPO.

Programmers, developers, and individuals introduced more digital assets to the marketplace. A new way to offer digital assets to the public soon became essential, leading to the birth of ICOs. ICOs began as the equivalent of IPOs but for coins, tokens, and other digital assets. During an ICO, the offeror gives out a new digital asset—such as tokens or cryptocurrencies—on their blockchain platform in exchange for established cryptocurrencies such as Bitcoin. ICOs offer a quick and inexpensive means for start-ups to access capital and grow their businesses without the burdens and costs of registration. An ICO differs from an "initial exchange offering" (IEO), which refers to token offerings through a cryptocurrency exchange available only to users of the exchange. While IEOs became popular in late 2019 after the launch of Binance Launchpad,[185] ICOs are now more common than IEOs. Despite their advantages, the SEC cautions investors about the potential for fraud, money laundering, and market manipulation in ICOs.[186] These dangers are prevalent because anyone with an idea for a coin or token, a computer with internet, and some cash can launch an ICO. These offerings are also less regulated than traditional IPOs and centralized financial activities. In fact, most ICOs are unregulated.

To understand what STOs are, you first need to understand the difference between a security token and a utility token. A security token is an ownership token whose value correlates to the company's value. A utility token offers a utility to its user; its value has no correlation to

185. BINANCE LAUNCHPAD, coinspeaker.com, (last visited April 22, 2022).
186. SEC, *Spotlight on Initial Coin Offerings (ICOs)* (2021), available at https://www.sec.gov/ICO

the company's value. An ICO launches utility tokens. An STO, on the other hand, launches security tokens. In short, an STO is a hybrid ICO and IPO—the blockchain lists its tokens (like with an ICO), but the tokens represent an ownership interest, such as the company's stocks (like with an IPO). STOs are cheaper than IPOs and are open only to institutional investors. See the chart below for a summary.

	IPO	ICO	IEO	STO
TYPE OF INVESTORS	Entire public	(Generally) entire public	Users of the exchange	Institutional investors
TYPE OF ISSUER	Public companies	Individuals; start-ups	Crypto-exchange companies	(Generally) public companies
OFFERING MATERIALS	Prospectus document	White paper	White paper	Prospectus document
ASSET TYPE	Traditional securities	Coin or token	Coin or token	Token backed by traditional security
PLATFORM	Registered stock exchange	(Generally) issuer's website	Crypto exchange itself	Registered stock exchange or crypto exchange
INVESTOR PROTECTION	High	Low	Medium-High	High
REGULATION	Highly regulated	Unregulated	Medium regulated	Highly regulated
RISK OF FRAUD	Low	High	Low-Medium	Low

FIRST OFFERING	The Bank of New York (known today as NY Mellon) held the first IPO in or about 1784.[187]	"MasterCoin," invented by J.R. Willett as a protocol to use Bitcoin Blockchain but with more options,[188] had the first ICO in mid-2013.	Binance held the first IEO in 2019 (sale of BitTorrent Tokens [BTT]) on its exchange platform, Binance Launchpad.[189]	In 2020, the SEC registered foreign blockchain company INX Limited, which held an STO with its $130 million token offering of INX tokens.[190]

Which offering is preferable depends on the facts of each individual case. Below are simplified examples of each type of offering:

- Example 1: Blackwell, Inc. has been operating for twenty years and has decided to go public with its shares. It completes its registration statement and prospectus. This is the traditional case with an IPO.

- Example 2: Mark wants to issue a new coin and develops a white paper that describes the coin, including its risks. He hopes to offer this coin as a form of digital money and payment method. Mark plans to offer the coin to the entire public all around the world. This is an ICO.

- Example 3: CryptoME, Co. is a new crypto exchange that plans to offer a token to its users. The exchange will act as the contributor and administrator of the token. This offering would be an IEO.

- Example 4: Jane owns LeFont, Inc. and develops a token to use within a closed ecosystem—only for her employees. The token will allow her employees to purchase company products and will function like an arcade token. The value of the tokens stems from their scarcity—supply and demand—and has nothing to do with the value of LeFont, Inc. This is a utility token that LeFont, Inc. can offer through an ICO.

187. STEHPANIE FARIS, *What Was the First Company Offered on the New York Stock* Exchange? finance.zacks.com, (May 3, 2019).
188. RUBEN MERRE, *ICO 101 — History of Initial Coin Off*erings (ICOs), medium.com, (May 22, 2019).
189. GERTRUDE CHAVEZ-DREYFUSS, *Explainer: Initial exchange offerings flourish in crypto market,* reuters.com, (Jun. 20, 2019).
190. RICHARD KASTELEIN, *INX Conducts First-Ever SEC-Registered Security Token Offering, McDermott Leads Round,* theblockchain.com, (Sep. 23, 2020).

- Example 5: Beaumont, LLC is a private company that plans to offer digital security tokens that comply with the federal securities laws and are sold on exchanges built on the blockchain. Beaumont offers the security token only to its institutional investors. This is an STO, sometimes called a "tokenized IPO."

Real-world offerings tend to be more nuanced than the above examples. The line drawn between SEC *registration* and SEC *exemption* is even finer. Blockchain and cryptocurrency attorneys must understand these differences, advantages and disadvantages, and consequences, and be able to explain these to clients considering an offering.

3. RISKS OF ICOS

Launching an ICO may seem easy. Compared to a traditional IPO, ICOs are cheaper, involve less formalities, and can reach individuals around the world. That said, a successful ICO is challenging. After the growth of ICOs in 2017 caught the SEC's eye, the ICO boom came to an abrupt stop. Today, ICO activity is again increasing steadily. Yet the SEC is showing no signs of slowing down its investigations into fraudulent ICO activity or unregistered ICOs. Below are a few examples of SEC-launched investigations in connection with ICOs:

Crowd Machine, Inc. and Metavine, Inc. and Founder

In January 2022, the SEC announced that it would bring charges against two companies and their founder, Australian citizen Craig Sproule (the defendants), for making false statements in connection with an unregistered offering of digital asset securities.[191] Sproule—referred to in social media as the "Man behind the Machine"—allegedly raised about $40.7 million through his companies in an ICO involving Crowd Machine Compute Tokens (CMCTs).

Sproule told investors that the proceeds from the ICO would be used to enable one of his companies' existing application-development software to operate on a decentralized network of users' own computers. But this plan never occurred. The defendants diverted over $5.8 million of proceeds from the ICO to gold-mining companies in South Africa. This was never disclosed to investors.

The SEC's investigation also alleged that the defendants knowingly sold their CMCTs to "ICO pools"—a group of investors—without determining whether those investors were accredited. The defendants offered and sold CMCTs through general solicitation efforts that included U.S. investors. These investors purchased CMCTs in exchange for either

191. SEC Press Release 2022-3, *SEC Charges ICO Issuer and Founder with Defrauding Investors*, sec.gov, (Jan. 6, 2022).

U.S. dollars or digital assets, such as Ether or Bitcoin. The offer and sale of the CMCTs resembled investment contracts and were therefore securities that needed to be registered or exempted under the federal securities laws.

The SEC emphasized the severity of the defendants' misleading representations to investors regarding how they were using the ICO proceeds, such as by spending the funds on a different scheme. The defendants consented to orders permanently enjoining them from further violations, which required that they disable the CMCT tokens and remove them from digital asset trading platforms, imposing a $195,047 civil penalty. The defendants will also be assessed for disgorgement, prejudgment interest, and civil penalties to be determined later by a court.

In the Matter of Blockchain of Things, Inc. (BCOT)

In late 2019, the SEC settled charges against start-up company BCOT for conducting an unregistered ICO of its digital tokens.[192] BCOT raised about $13 million from its ICO and had planned to use the funds for its future business plans, which included developing its blockchain technology and platform. BCOT had emphasized that the platform would allow third-party developers to build applications for message transmission and digital-asset activities.

Central to the SEC's investigation was its allegation that BCOT sold digital tokens to U.S. investors and worked with four resellers that would be the exclusive sellers of BCOT's digital tokens in specified foreign countries with no resale restrictions. Under the *Howey* Test, the SEC determined that an investor or purchaser in the BCOT token offering would have expected to make a profit in the future based on BCOT's efforts to develop an ecosystem for users on its platform—including the use of the ICO proceeds to control and enhance the value of the BCOT tokens. This conduct was carried out without proper registration or an applicable exemption. The SEC noted that it was pertinent that BCOT did not provide its investors with important information needed for a security offering.

Along with a cease-and-desist order, BCOT was fined $250,000. The SEC required that BCOT return all funds to investors who had bought its token in the ICO. BCOT announced plans to properly register its tokens as securities and comply with the various disclosure and reporting requirements.

192. SEC Press Release 2019-267, *Issuer Settles Unregistered ICO Charges, Agrees to Return Funds and Register Tokens,* sec.gov, (Dec. 18, 2019).

In the Matter of BitClave, PTE Ltd.

In mid-2020, the SEC released a press release on its investigation into blockchain-services company BitClave for conduct dating to 2017.[193] The investigation involved an unregistered ICO of digital-asset securities. For six months, BitClave had sold its Consumer Activity Tokens (CAT) to about 9,500 investors and raised over $25 million. BitClave had planned to use the proceeds of the ICO to develop a blockchain-based search platform for targeted consumer advertising.

The SEC tracked several factors that revealed BitClave was selling securities. BitClave observed how its tokens would increase in value and took active steps to ensure that the tokens could be tradeable on third-party platforms after the ICO was completed. Also, purchasers of the CAT token could have reasonably expected to make a profit by selling the tokens after the token distribution. Based on the *Howey* Test and the evidence gathered and reviewed, the SEC determined that this was a clear case of unregistered securities.

BitClave agreed to return the proceeds received from the offering as well as pay additional monetary relief to a Fair Fund to be distributed to investors. Financially, the SEC's order involved disgorgement of $25,500,000, prejudgment interest of $3,444,197, and a penalty of $400,000. BitClave has since announced its intention to wind down operations and stop the development of its platform.

In the Matter of Block.one

In 2019, the SEC settled charges against blockchain-technology company Block.one for conducting an unregistered offering of its digital tokens.[194] The offering raised several billion dollars over about one year—between June 2017 and June 2018. Block.one, which had operations in Virginia and Hong Kong, promised to use the funds from the ICO for general expenses and to develop software and promote blockchains. Block.one offered and sold 900 million digital tokens that were neither registered with the SEC nor qualified for an exemption from registration.

The SEC made this determination by reviewing the *Howey* Test. Here, a purchaser of the token would expect to make a future profit derived from Block.one's efforts. These efforts included developing the software as well as promoting the software and launching the anticipated blockchains. The SEC's order required Block.one to pay a $24 million civil monetary penalty.

---

193. SEC Press Release 2020-124, *Unregistered $25.5 Million ICO Issuer to Return Money for Distribution to Investors,* sec.gov, (May 28, 2020).
194. SEC Press Release 2019-202, *SEC Orders Blockchain Company to Pay $24 Million Penalty for Unregistered ICO,* sec.gov, (Sept. 30, 2019).

In the Matter of Gladius Network, LLC

The SEC charged Gladius with conducting an unregistered ICO in late 2017 that raised about $12.7 million in digital assets—GLA tokens.[195] After applying the *Howey* Test, a purchaser would have a reasonable expectation of making a profit based on the efforts of Gladius to create a marketplace from the sale of the GLA tokens and provide investors with liquidity by making the GLA tokens tradeable on secondary markets. The offering was not registered with nor exempted by the Commission.

The funds from the offering were to be used to finance a network for renting spare computer bandwidth. In mid-2018, Gladius self-reported to the SEC to cooperate with the investigation and take remedial steps. Because of Gladius's self-reporting, agreement to compensate investors, and commitment to register the tokens as securities, the SEC did not impose a penalty.

In the Matter of Tierion, Inc.

In this administrative proceeding issued in late 2020, the SEC settled charges against a blockchain start-up from Texas, Tierion, in connection with an unregistered offering of its tokens.[196] In July 2017, Tierion raised about $25 million from the sale of its Tierion Network Tokens (TNT). The SEC's order concluded that Tierion had told its investors that the proceeds from the offering would be used to fund the development of the Tierion Network. This Network would offer various blockchain services.

The SEC concluded that Tierion had issued securities in violation of the federal registration provisions. A purchaser would have held a reasonable expectation of obtaining a future profit based on the statements made by Tierion that it would use the proceeds from the ICO to continue developing the Tierion Network. Tierion had also stated that these development efforts would allow it to add partners, infrastructure, and services. The SEC determined that TNT are securities and that Tierion did not register the tokens nor comply with an applicable exemption.

The settlement required that Tierion pay a $250,000 penalty, stop the trading of the TNTs, and return funds to the investors who had purchased tokens from the offering or in the secondary market, who had received TNT as a reward from Tierion, and who had bought TNT and later sold it at a loss.

195. SEC Press Release 2019-15, *Company Settles Unregistered ICO Charges After Self-Reporting to SEC,* sec.gov, (Feb. 20, 2019).

196. SEC Administrative Proceeding File No. 3-20188, *Issuer of Unregistered $25 Million ICO Settles with SEC,* sec.gov, (Dec. 23, 2020).

SEC Enforcement Summary. As shown by these example cases, the SEC has continued to investigate ICO activity since 2017 and will not discriminate whether the defendant is an individual, small group of people, blockchain start-up, service company, or large business. Usually, the entities and persons will receive a civil penalty but may also be assessed for disgorgement, prejudgment interest, injunctions, and cease-and-desist orders. The costs and reputational harm can be so significant that the entity is forced to wind down operations after the SEC's investigation. Those fortunate enough to continue operations have had to transform their operations. Besides registering—or proceeding with an applicable registration exemption—these companies will have to comply with the stringent, periodic reporting and disclosure requirements under the Exchange Act of 1934.

SUMMARY

Companies continue to turn to blockchain-dependent offerings such as ICOs because of their reduced cost and ease of reaching investors around the world. But the 2017 spike in ICO activity did not last long. After federal agencies such as the SEC saw the value of cryptocurrencies soar, it turned its attention to scrutinizing various ICOs and blockchain start-ups. As a result, companies are now choosing the SEC seal of approval given with STOs. The tokens issued with STOs—security tokens—offer the flexibility of reaching individuals around the world without fear of an SEC enforcement action or private claim for unregistered securities. But this decision has not been easy and included failed ICO attempts or ICOs that led to enforcement actions. Besides enforcement cases initiated by the SEC, private actors have also filed complaints against companies for conduct as part of unregistered ICOs or fraudulent ICO activity.

§ 10 Private Enforcement

Blockchain and smart contracts will impact private litigation. Although digital-asset technology is new, the private litigant's legal remedies are not. A private litigant's satchel of remedies includes traditional breach of contract, common law fraud, and intellectual property causes of action. Programmers, developers, entities, and individuals involved with digital-asset undertakings may be subject to civil-lawsuit challenges.

1. CLAIMANTS AND LEGAL CLAIMS

Private-action plaintiffs include crypto buyers and sellers, online crypto exchanges, private investors, institutional investors, banks using crypto, miners, crypto developers and programmers, and other blockchain/DeFi-related companies. Interestingly, the defendants in these lawsuits fall into the same categories. While private claimants may proceed individually, these lawsuits are usually styled as class actions. Here are the most common private claimant causes of action:

POTENTIAL CAUSES OF ACTION
Claimants may rely on a variety of traditional legal claims, including: (1) breach of contract, (2) breach of fiduciary duty, (3) whether the asset is a security, (4) common-law fraud, negligence, and tort, (5) antitrust and competition violations, (6) employment-law violations, (7) false advertising and misrepresentation, (8) intellectual-property issues, (9) trademark infringement, (10) privacy-law matters; (11) computer crimes such as hacking, (12) token valuation, and (13) market manipulation.

Certain of these causes of action (for example, securities fraud; whether the asset is a security) are federal, but most lawsuits involve state common law and are brought in state court.

A primary remedy for private lawsuits is rescission—the unwinding of the entire sale. For example, Company X launches an ICO and issues a new token to the international public without registering with the SEC.

After Company X raises $10 million, the investors allege fraud in the solicitation process. The Securities Act of 1933 makes individuals who control an entity personally liable for the sale of unregistered securities. If the claimants succeed, the court could unwind the sale and require the issuer to give back every dollar it raised. But these claims suffer from one drawback: the statute of limitations is short. Under Section 13 of the Securities Act, claims alleging unregistered securities must be filed within one year of the date of the violation. The one-year statute can be problematic for claimants because many ICO-related violations occurred in 2017 or 2018, before the SEC's published framework on digital assets. Although a case alleging unregistered securities cannot be filed outside the one-year period, the purchasers may proceed with other causes of action under state and federal law for fraud and misstatements.

Private litigation in the digital-asset-undertaking arena will likely increase in both number and intensity, especially where there is fuel from major private players. For instance, Jack Dorsey's Square has a more than $200-million corporate stake in Bitcoin, and Elon Musk's Tesla has bought about $1.5 billion in Bitcoin.[197]

2. PRIVATE LITIGATION AND ICOS

In November 2021, a significant development in cryptocurrency jurisprudence occurred. For the first time, a jury decided whether a cryptocurrency or digital asset was a "security." The verdict? The cryptocurrency products were not securities under the *Howey* Test.

This class-action lawsuit, *Audet vs. Fraser*,[198] began in 2016 when a class of investors and purchasers sued several executives and companies involved in the sale of the cryptocurrency token "Hashlets." The class alleged that the defendants, including GAW Miners, defrauded plaintiffs and contravened the federal securities laws through the offer and sale of unregistered securities.

The defendants collected about $19 million in revenue from investors. At first, the defendants sold Hashlets contracts, which equaled shares of profits that the investors were entitled to from GAW's mining profits. When the defendants could no longer support the Hashlets, they began selling "Hashpoints"—promissory notes that individuals could buy or mine and then convert into a forthcoming virtual currency called "Paycoin." The investors would hold Paycoin in digital wallets called "HashStakers" and supposedly earn a daily payout. The class alleged

197. ROBERT ANELLO, *Crypto Goes Corporate: Litigation Sure to Follow*, forbes.com, (May 26, 2021).

198. *Audet v. Fraser*, No. 3:16-CV-940, ECF No. 57 at 6, (D. Conn. 2021); *Audet v. Fraser*, No. 3:16-CV-940 (MPS) (D. Conn. Oct. 11, 2017); *Audet v. Garza*, 3:16-CV-940, (D. Conn. Jun. 15, 2016).

that the Hashlets, Hashpoints, HashStakers, and Paycoin contracts were investment contracts, and that their offer and sale constituted an unregistered offering in violation of federal securities laws. The class also asserted state-law violations, common-law fraud, and common-law aiding-and-abetting fraud, among other claims.

Not only was the jury's verdict significant, but the court's instructions on the contours of the *Howey* Test were also noteworthy. The court instructed the jury that the analysis for each element had to focus on what the purchasers *reasonably* expected. Respecting a common enterprise, the instruction focused on whether the purchasers' profits correlated to either (i) the profits of other purchasers by pooling their assets proportionately to the purchasers' investments, or (ii) GAW's profits. Either of these factors would satisfy the common-enterprise requirement. The court grouped the last two elements together and noted that the jury:

> [S]hould consider whether the product was being promoted primarily as an investment, in which case it would be an investment contract, or whether the product was being promoted as a means whereby participants could pool their activities, money, and the promoter's contribution in a meaningful way, in which case it would not be an investment contract. If there was a reasonable expectation of significant investor control, then profits would not be considered derived solely from the efforts of others. But if the expectation was that the participants would be passive investors, then profits would be considered derived solely from the efforts of others. The touchstone is the presence of an investment in a common venture premised on a reasonable expectation of profits to be derived from the entrepreneurial or managerial efforts of others.[199]

This instruction is broad and appears to be defendant friendly. By adding the "reasonable" expectation of "significant" investor control, the court tipped the analysis in the defendants' favor, if they could show that the investors expected to retain significant control or that their profit expectations were unreasonable under the circumstances. With GAW, the jury found that none of its crypto-related products were investment contracts and were therefore not securities.

The *Audet* court's expansion of "currency" beyond "fiat currencies" was also noteworthy. The Exchange Act of 1934 includes an exception to the definition of "securities" for currencies. Even if the digital asset satisfies the definition of an investment contract, it is still not a security if it is a currency. The GAW defendants claimed that its products were virtual currencies and thus not securities.

---

199. *Audet v. Fraser*, No. 3:16-CV-00940-MPS, (D. Conn. Oct. 29, 2021).

The *Audet* court's instructions made clear that classifying an item of value as a currency is insufficient. The jury must rather focus on the substance and economic realities of the digital asset. Under these instructions, digital assets that satisfy each element of *Howey* can still escape registration requirements if the asset is a currency. But proving that the digital asset is a currency conflicts with IRS guidance. The IRS does not classify cryptocurrencies as legal tender but considers them to be "property." The *Audet* court's instructions may still serve as a useful starting point for courts to determine whether digital assets are securities.

As a final example, in *StormsMedia, LLC vs. Giga Watt, Inc.*, the plaintiffs launched a putative class action against Giga Watt, Inc. alleging that the defendants' ICO of newly issued tokens was in fact a securities offering.[200] The plaintiffs claimed that in anticipation of the defendants' plans to launch a cryptocurrency-mining facility, Giga Watt held an ICO inviting investors to contribute either cryptocurrencies (for example, Bitcoin or Ether) or U.S. dollars in exchange for (1) Giga Watt's token, called "WTT," which would give investors the right to use Giga Watt's Bitcoin-mining software rent free for fifty years, or (2) Bitcoin-mining equipment. According to the plaintiffs, the defendants represented that the token's value (then around $1.00 to $1.20 per token) would increase based on the success of Giga Watt's operations. For the investors that chose the Bitcoin-mining equipment, implementation and hosting would be at Giga Watt's facility. The plaintiffs' aggregate contributions were about $100 million.

The class-action complaint alleged that through the ICO, the plaintiffs contributed to Giga Watt's common enterprise with the expectation that Giga Watt's efforts would increase the value of their investments and provide a return on investment. The class requested rescission—the return of their invested funds—under Section 12(a)(1) of the Securities Act. Section 12(a)(1) gives investors the right to recover the consideration paid, with interest, from any person who offers or sells a security in violation of the federal securities laws' registration requirements, without showing fraud. The case ended after only a few months when Giga Watt settled with the lead plaintiff, who then voluntarily dismissed the lawsuit without prejudice.

The Giga Watt case exposes the rising trend of plaintiffs alleging unregistered securities offerings involving digital assets. Investors are educating themselves on the definition of a security, the requirements of SEC registration, the exemptions from registration, and their rights under Section 12(a)(1). Although the Giga Watt case ended quickly, it

200. *StormsMedia, LLC v. Giga Watt, Inc.*, 2:17-CV-00438, (E.D. Wash. Dec. 28, 2017).

was a prime example to issuers that if they do not register their token-funded offering or meet an exemption, they may face liability for selling unregistered securities. Some issuers have tried to insulate themselves from this risk by stating in their white papers that they have conducted an internal analysis and determined that their offering does not constitute a security for registration purposes. But this disclaimer has been found insufficient, as discussed below.

The above cases show that there is no consensus on whether digital assets are securities, particularly because individuals can use, create, market, and distribute each digital asset differently. The only certainty is that whether a product, contract, or arrangement is an investment contract will depend on the facts of each case.

One may ask why these lawsuits focus on unregistered securities rather than asserting Rule 10b-5 fraud claims. The answer lies in the difference between traditional markets for IPO trading and the markets that facilitate ICOs. A Rule 10b-5 case requires that the plaintiff proves reliance on the issuer's material misstatements or omissions. Meeting this requirement is challenging in a class action because it is next to impossible to prove reliance for every class member. Therefore courts developed the "Fraud on the Market" (FOTM) theory. FOTM theory presumes that stock-market prices contain all material information available to investors and that investors can rely on this information. If the plaintiffs plead that fraud modified the market price and that this modification caused plaintiffs to either buy or sell, reliance is established. The U.S. Supreme Court stated as follows on the FOTM theory:

FOTM THEORY
Such a presumption relieves the Rule 10b-5 plaintiff of an unrealistic evidentiary burden and reflects, and is supportive of, the Act's policy of requiring full disclosure and fostering reliance on market integrity. The presumption is also supported by common sense and probability: An investor who trades stock at the price set by an impersonal market does so relying on the integrity of that price. Because most publicly available information is reflected in market price, an investor's reliance on any public material misrepresentations may be presumed for purposes of a Rule 10b-5 action.[201]

While the FOTM theory enables class actions to proceed with Rule 10b-5 claims,[202] the problem is that the theory depends on efficient market trading. Cryptocurrency activity and ICO trading do not occur on efficient markets. Instead, they occur on inefficient, volatile, and unregulated markets—online and often unregistered—including cryptocurrency exchanges or platforms. Thus, few Rule 10b-5 allegations survive in

201. *Basic, Inc. v. Levinson*, 485 U.S. 224, 225, (1988).
202. *Id.* at 224.

connection with ICOs, resulting in frequent allegations of unregistered securities offerings.

3. DIGITAL ASSETS AND CLASS-ACTION LAWSUITS

In 2020, there was a boom in private class-action lawsuits filed in the Southern District of New York against several online crypto exchanges and entities: four against crypto asset exchanges (Binance, Bibox, KuCoin, and HDR Global Trading, Ltd.—operating BitMEX), and seven against issuers of crypto tokens (Tron Foundation, Block.one, Civic Technologies, Inc., KayDex Pty Ltd., Quantstamp, Inc., Status Research & Development GmbH, and BProtocol Foundation). These lawsuits share many characteristics.

First, each began as a class-action lawsuit. Class actions are useful vehicles for bringing claims where there are many injured investors—often dispersed around the nation (or even the world)—in a single lawsuit against the same defendant(s).

Second, these lawsuits alleged that the defendants engaged in the sale of unregistered securities under Sections 5 and 12(a)(1) of the Securities Act of 1933.

Third, the complaints alleged that some defendants were conducting broker activities without heeding the proper registration procedures, thereby violating Sections 15(a)(1) and 29(b) of the Exchange Act of 1934.

Fourth, the classes in certain actions asserted violations of the Commodities Exchange Act and state blue-sky laws (that is, state laws regulating the offering and sale of securities).

Fifth, the classes alleged fraud stemming from the omission of information needed for the purchasers to make an informed investment decision (for example, risk exposure). On top of the material omissions, several of the defendants' white papers affirmatively stated that the issued tokens were not securities under the federal securities laws.

Sixth, the classes alleged losses directly caused by some defendants' misleading statements about the offering, coin, or token opportunity. For example, certain defendants promised investment returns, but the ICOs instead led to significant losses for the investors.

Seventh, the classes alleged that the defendants exploited the novelty of ICO offerings and the technology in 2017 and 2018 to gain a financial advantage from the coin or token offerings.

Defendants are raising defenses based on the statute of limitations and personal jurisdiction. In particular, the statute of limitations for Section 12(a)(1) claims is one year. Several defendants are foreign entities that held their ICOs on foreign exchanges, thus raising personal-jurisdiction issues.

This 2020 wave of class-action lawsuits pertained to conduct *before* the SEC released its guidance on cryptocurrencies and tokens. Recall that the SEC did not publish its "Framework for 'Investment Contract' Analysis of Digital Assets"[203] until 2019. This framework has assisted the SEC, issuing entities, and investors determine whether a digital-asset offering will be treated as an investment contract under Howey and thus a security subject to the registration and ongoing reporting and disclosure requirements under the federal securities laws. Holding the above plaintiffs to the one-year statute-of-limitations period while ignoring the lack of SEC guidance before 2019 seems counterintuitive to fairness and transparency.

These class-action lawsuits show that investors are aware of both the law and their rights when investing in new technologies. If they believe they have been harmed in a crypto-related venture, private claimants will not hesitate to sue issuers for securities-law violations, inadequate disclosures, and opportunistic behavior at the expense of investors. Investors are heeding SEC enforcement actions, which can spur the commencement of private lawsuits.

Two older seminal class action lawsuits, BitConnect and Tezos, provide more instruction and warrant brief discussion.

In the beginning of 2018, three putative classes of investors sued BitConnect's three corporate entities and their representatives in connection with BitConnect's cryptocurrency—the BitConnect coin (BCC).[204] After BCC launched in 2016, investors bought BCC with other cryptocurrencies (such as Bitcoin) and then lent the BCCs back to BitConnect in exchange for interest payouts based on the size of their purchase/loan. About two years later, BCC's market capitalization hit around $2.7 billion. The classes alleged that BitConnect achieved this capitalization by orchestrating an elaborate Ponzi scheme involving the solicitation of investments with a guaranteed daily return of up to 40%, regardless of market performance.

The plaintiffs alleged that BitConnect induced investors to purchase BCCs by claiming that it would achieve the promised returns using its own trading bot and volatility software. BitConnect achieved these "returns" by using the investments of new and former investors.

203. SEC, *Framework for "Investment Contract" Analysis of Digital Assets*, seq.gov, (2019), available at https://www.sec.gov/corpfin/framework-investment-contract-analysis-digital-assets

204. *Wildes v. BitConnect Intl. PLC*, No. 9:18-CV-80086-DMM, (S.D. Fla, Jan. 24, 2018).

After state securities regulators demanded that BitConnect cease operations, BitConnect closed in January 2018. These regulators—as well as countries including the United Kingdom, Singapore, India, and Australia—issued warnings to investors about the scam, and the BCC became worthless.

In another class-action lawsuit, the putative class sued BitConnect for the sale of unregistered securities, conversion, conspiracy, violation of state consumer-protection statutes, fraud, and breach of contract. The class alleged losses of over $770,000 and sought rescission of their contractual agreements with BitConnect. While the federal court dismissed the lawsuit in 2020, the BitConnect story was far from over. Several other lawsuits were filed against BitConnect in multiple U.S. states as well as around the world, and various federal agencies also got involved.

For instance, the FBI created a program to find the victims of the BitConnect scheme.[205] Additionally, in November 2021, the DOJ seized about $56 million in fraudulent cryptocurrency proceeds.[206] This seizure represented the largest cryptocurrency-fraud recovery in history, and the funds will be used to compensate victims of the BitConnect fraud. The SEC also charged (i) the founder of BitConnect with securities fraud for his role in fraudulently raising over $2 billion from investors and (ii) a BitConnect promoter and his firm with fraudulently receiving over $24 million in referral commissions.[207] Under 18 U.S. Code § 1348, a person commits securities fraud under these circumstances:

> Whoever knowingly executes, or attempts to execute, a scheme or artifice (1) to defraud any person in connection with any commodity for future delivery, or any option on a commodity for future delivery, or any security of an issuer . . .; or (2) to obtain, by means of false or fraudulent pretenses, representations, or promises, any money or property in connection with the purchase or sale of any commodity for future delivery, or any option on a commodity for future delivery, or any security of an issuer . . . shall be fined under this title, or imprisoned not more than twenty-five years, or both.[208]

In *Tezos*, five class actions were filed against Dynamic Ledger Solutions, Inc. (DLS), its founders and representatives, and its affiliate,

205. FBI, *Seeking Victims in BitConnect Investigation,* fbi.gov, (Feb. 12, 2019).
206. DOJ NEWS, *$56 Million in Seized Cryptocurrency Being Sold as First Step to Compensate Victims of BitConnect Fraud Scheme*, justice.gov, (Nov. 16, 2021).
207. SEC Press Release 2021-172, *SEC Charges Global Crypto Lending Platform and Top Executives in $2 Billion Fraud,* sec.gov, (Sept. 1, 2021).
208. 18 U.S.C. Code § 1348.

Tezos Foundation.[209] Tezos was a Swiss nonprofit entity that raised funds to help purchase DLS on the Tezos network. Individuals who donated their cryptocurrencies received rights in Tezos's cryptocurrency—"Tezzies"—which defendants promoted as a cryptocurrency to compete with Bitcoin.

In 2017, DLS and Tezos's founders held an ICO in which they allegedly made multiple false promises to investors to induce purchases of rights in Tezzies. The ICO raised about $232 million in Bitcoin and Ether, which at the time was the largest ICO. Investors in the class-action lawsuit alleged that the Tezzie rights bought as part of the ICO constituted unregistered securities entitling them to rescission under Sections 5, 12, and 15 of the Securities Act of 1933. The class also alleged several state-laws claims, including violations of consumer protection statutes and unfair and deceptive practices. After years of litigation, discovery, and mediation, Tezos settled for $25 million.

The above cases highlight several trends in digital-asset litigation. First, private litigation can motivate government-initiated investigations, as shown by the SEC, FBI, and DOJ's actions following the start of the *BitConnect* class-action lawsuit. Second, private litigation can replace government enforcement, as shown by the *Tezos* defendants' attempt to avoid an SEC enforcement action by quickly settling the litigation. Third, issues relating to personal jurisdiction in digital-asset class actions are likely to increase, as private claimants may find it difficult to prove that securities traded on a domestic exchange or involved a domestic transaction.

The days where individuals who dabble in crypto investments are without recourse when an investment falls through are over. Token sales are no longer the Wild West of Fintech. The law, investor knowledge and action, and federal agency enforcement are beginning to catch up to these unprecedented technologies. Multiple efforts at regulation have begun and will continue to ensue. Investors, businesses, and the SEC are aware of ICOs. But a consistent and reliable means of regulation and enforcement is lacking. For now, issuers engaging in an offering of a digital asset that is a security may face an SEC enforcement action or a private lawsuit.

4. DIGITAL ASSETS AND INTELLECTUAL PROPERTY LAW

Intellectual-property disputes in the digital-asset arena are not limited to copyrights, trademarks, and trade secrets. Digital-asset disputes can implicate a wide range of issues, including brand dilution,

209. *In Re Tezos Securities Litigation*, No. 3:17-CV-06779-RS, (N.D. Cal.).

misappropriation, unfair and deceptive practices, breach of contract, intentional interference with contracts, conversion, and unjust enrichment. The few cases discussed below involve cryptocurrency exchanges, blockchain technology, and intellectual property violations, proving the range of possibilities.

The first case, filed in 2020 by Ripple Labs, Inc., and its CEO Brad Garlinghouse against YouTube, involved trademark infringement, violation of the right of publicity, and unfair and fraudulent business practices under state law.[210] Ripple Labs, a private blockchain-technology company that aims to facilitate the transfer of money anywhere in the word, uses its cryptocurrency, XRP, to facilitate cross-border payments. Mr. Garlinghouse was the public face of the company. YouTube's terms of service prohibit, among other things, scams or other deceptive practices that may harm users (for example, advertising offering cash gifts or get-rich-quick schemes). YouTube allegedly failed to stop a fraudulent scheme in 2019 involving XRP.

According to Ripple Labs, a group of unknown scammers used YouTube accounts to impersonate Ripple and Mr. Garlinghouse. Using fake channels and advertisements that impersonated official Ripple Labs channels, the scammers promised individuals that they would receive a windfall in return for transferring their XRP— which some users did. Ripple Labs alleged that despite over 350 takedown notices sent to YouTube, users' YouTube warnings, and media coverage on "the XRP Giveaway Scam," YouTube failed to stop and punish the scammers, thereby contributing to the scammers' trademark infringement. In response, YouTube claimed that (a) it lacked knowledge of the scam, and (b) as an interactive computer service (and not a "publisher" or "speaker"), it should be immune from Ripple Lab's state-law claims under Section 230 of the Communications Decency Act.

The court dismissed Ripple Lab's claims. They found that YouTube's delays in responding did not amount to contributory trademark infringement. Ripple Lab failed to submit evidence that YouTube had contemporaneous knowledge of the infringing conduct while continuing to supply its services, and it insufficiently pled constructive knowledge. The court held that YouTube is not an online marketplace that monitors its vendors, but only a social-media platform that hosts users' content. Thus, YouTube's responsibility to police hackers is different than if it were an online marketplace. Finally, although Ripple Labs asserted that YouTube contributed to the scam by verifying the responsible YouTube accounts, the court held that the scam involved only the posted videos, not the verification process.

---

210. *Ripple Labs Inc v. YouTube LLC*, 2020 WL 6822891, (N.D. Cal. Nov. 20, 2020).

In the second case, *Nowak vs. Xapo, Inc.*, plaintiff Nowak alleged that the online exchanges Xapo and Indodax aided and abetted the theft of 500 bitcoins that Nowak had deposited in his U.S.-based exchange account.[211] The complaint alleged that Xapo and Indodax had violated federal law and California's Computer Data Access and Fraud Act (CDAFA, also known as the Anti-Hacking Statute—a criminal provision that prohibits access to computers, computer systems, and networks without permission to do harm or engage in unauthorized use) by aiding an unknown individual's unauthorized access to a computer and theft of the Bitcoins.

According to Nowak, the defendant exchanges knew they had weak AML/KYC policies and therefore enabled the criminal activity to persist. Nowak requested the return of his Bitcoins, which were worth about $2.3 million at the time of the theft. The court dismissed the plaintiff's CDAFA claim because (a) the plaintiff failed to show that the exchanges engaged in or had the requisite knowledge of the hacking activity, and (b) the defendants' constructive knowledge of their allegedly inadequate security systems could not maintain a claim.

The third case arose in October 2019, when Finco Services, Inc.—which operated under the name "Current"—sued Facebook, Inc., Calibra, Inc., JLV, LLC, and Character SF, LLC for trademark infringement, unfair competition, false designation of origin under Section 43(a) of the Lanham Act, and various state-law claims.[212] Calibra is a subsidiary of Facebook that was planning to launch a new digital currency called "Libra." The action involved the defendants' alleged unauthorized use of the plaintiff's trademarks and service marks in the marketing, promotion, and advertising of the defendants' Calibra digital-wallet service.

In 2016, Current hired defendant Character, a branding and design agency, to develop a logo and branding strategy for Current's mobile app and banking services. Current registered its logo with the U.S. Patent and Trademark Office (USPTO) for several purposes, including for a mobile software application that facilitated cryptocurrency transactions, and began using the logo in 2016. In 2018, Facebook announced the launch of Calibra and hired Character to do the branding and marketing campaign. The plaintiff alleged that Character created a logo design for Calibra that was almost identical to, created confusion with, and infringed on the design Character had created for Current. Below is a side-by-side comparison of the two logos found in paragraph 36 of the complaint:

---

211. *Nowak v. Xapo, Inc.*, 20-CV-3643, (Jun. 1, 2020).
212. *Finco Services, Inc. v. Facebook Inc.*, 1:19-CV-09410, (Oct. 10, 2019).

When Current approached the general counsel of Calibra and Facebook about the two logos, they did nothing. Finco/Current then filed the lawsuit, seeking treble damages, punitive damages, attorneys' fees, pre- and post-judgment interest, and an order enjoining defendants from using the logo. After the lawsuit was filed, Facebook renamed its digital wallet from Calibra to "Novi."[213]

The new design was created to remove the similarities and alleviate any confusion between Current's logo and Calibra's logo. Whether the name change and logo modification are sufficient, or whether the "O" infringes Current's logo, remains unsettled.

Intellectual-property cases involving blockchain technology and cryptocurrency are like traditional intellectual-property cases because digital assets—whether a new token, ICO, or other form of digital asset—are the property of the individual or entity that created or developed them. These assets, like any other property, are therefore protected against infringement and other intellectual-property violations.

Examples of protected assets include a firm's newly issued cryptocurrency or token, as well its CEO's name and likeness. The level of protection afforded to these assets depends on the nature of the entity's business. Courts may continue to find a distinction between (1) technology providers or platforms that host content for their users and (2) online marketplaces that facilitate trades between vendors. As shown in *Ripple Labs*, the former is treated as an intermediary that does not have the same strict duties of reacting to suspicious conduct as the latter.

Nowak presents a similar situation. The court made it clear that the defendant's exchange could not be liable for aiding theft based on mere allegations of weak AML/KYC policies. The plaintiff had to prove that the exchange engaged in the hacking itself or knew about the hacking before its completion. Thus, the court required overt action or direct

213. DAVID MARCUS, *Welcome to Novi*, about.fb.com, (May 26, 2020).

knowledge—similar to what the court required for the video-sharing platform YouTube—to implicate the applicable regulatory intellectual-property provisions and entitle the claimant to relief.

Another notable development highlighted in *Nowak* was that the plaintiff hired a private investigator to trace his Bitcoins. Future claimants may follow this new approach to crypto-related investigations and hire their own firms to bolster their cases. These new crypto-tracing attempts will indirectly result in the erosion of anonymity from crypto transactions.

More crypto-related services and apps will likely emerge. Intellectual-property differentiation will therefore be critical to standing out in the marketplace—and avoiding lawsuits. As seen in *Finco*, Current's logo would not differentiate its app because Facebook, with its unparalleled presence in the marketplace, had a similar logo. Thus, Current had to sue for trademark infringement to receive the full benefit of its logo. Logos for cryptocurrency products and services help users visually identify the product/service with a particular company. With these apps launching at an exponential rate, more trademark-infringement lawsuits are inevitable.

For example, assume online content platforms ChatSpace, Inc. and Talk & Click, Co. have similar logos for their services or mobile apps. While an infringement claim may turn on which company had the logo first, whether the public noticed the similarities will also be relevant. On the other hand, if Twitter introduces a blockchain-powered app that uses a logo design almost identical to a logo used by ChatSpace for five years, public confusion is more likely to arise. Twitter would not want the negative publicity to interfere with the launch of its new app—similar to how Facebook wanted to prevent Current's trademark-infringement lawsuit from interfering with Facebook's new Libra cryptocurrency. In fact, Facebook not only delayed the launch of its coin partly because of Current's trademark-infringement lawsuit, but it also prompted them to introduce both a new design and a different name.

While intellectual-property lawsuits involving cryptocurrency services and blockchain-related issues involve new and emerging technologies, these lawsuits still tend to follow the same approach as traditional intellectual-property lawsuits. Thus, it is important not to forget the fundamental tenets and practices of intellectual-property law and litigation.

5. DIGITAL ASSETS AND ANTITRUST LAW

Antitrust law is concerned with fair competition and the prevention of monopolies, price fixing, boycotts, and similar restraints on trade. But where do cryptocurrency transactions and blockchain companies come into play?

The power that comes with cryptocurrencies and blockchain technologies can bring with it greed and corruption. In mid-October 2021, the total market capitalization of cryptocurrencies reached an all-time high of $2 trillion. Unfortunately, companies and individuals in positions of authority often abuse their power by engaging in collusion or other anti-competitive behavior.

Antitrust issues have arisen under Section 1 of the Sherman Act and Section 16 of the Clayton Act. Section 1 of the Sherman Act provides that every contract, combination in the form of trust, or conspiracy in restraint of trade or commerce is illegal. Section 16 of the Clayton Act authorizes any person or entity to seek injunctive relief against threatened loss or damage caused by violations of the antitrust laws. Although scholars may debate whether antitrust law applies to non-regulated industries such as cryptocurrencies or blockchain technology, the cases below establish that claimants are already bringing lawsuits alleging anticompetitive behavior.

United American Corp. vs. Bitmain, Inc.[214] was the first time a private party sued over antitrust violations involving cryptocurrencies and blockchain technology. Filed in December 2018, this suit became known as the "Bitcoin Cash Hijack Lawsuit." The case began with the hard fork of the Bitcoin Cash Blockchain in November 2018. Recall that Bitcoin Cash resulted from a "hard fork" from the original Bitcoin Blockchain. Any time a blockchain undergoes an update, that change creates either a soft fork or a hard fork. A soft fork involves a change to the software protocol that is backward compatible. Only one blockchain will remain valid after the software update. A hard fork involves a radical upgrade that leads to a permanent chain separation and two blockchains. It is *not* backward compatible; validators on the network must upgrade to the newer version for their transactions and blocks to remain valid.[215]

The *Bitmain* case involved two Bitcoin-mining companies: plaintiff United American Corp. and defendant Bitmain. Bitcoin Cash was undergoing a planned hard fork in November 2018. At the time, there were two competing proposals for the fork: the ABC protocol and the SV protocol. The prevailing protocol would be the one that had the most hashing power—whichever had the most mining energy to mine a cryptocurrency. The plaintiff alleged that the defendant colluded with

214. *United American Corp. v. Bitmain, Inc.*, No. 1:2018-CV-25106, (S.D. Fla., Dec. 6, 2018).

215. *Soft Fork v. Hard Fork: Differences Explained*, cointelegraph.com, available at https://cointelegraph.com/blockchain-for-beginners/soft-fork-vs-hard-fork-differences-explained

others in a hijacking scheme to support the ABC protocol. The ABC fork won the contest and became the new and official Bitcoin Cash Blockchain. The plaintiff used mining services tailored for Bitcoin Cash SV, and its profits corresponded to that protocol. The selection of the ABC protocol led to significant losses for the plaintiff. In fact, the combined values of the protocols plummeted. In its complaint, the plaintiff alleged that the defendant and others conspired to use their hashing power in a centralized way that promoted the ABC protocol even though blockchains are supposed to be decentralized.

The antitrust issues presented included: 1) whether the defendant and others in the Bitcoin Cash ABC group conspired to restrain trade, and 2) whether this restraint on trade caused an injury to the plaintiff cognizable under antitrust law. The plaintiff argued that by making centralized checkpoints, the group had destroyed the decentralized nature of blockchains, which constituted an anticompetitive move. The defendant moved to dismiss, arguing that the plaintiff had failed to provide evidence of an agreement between the defendant and others, and that there was no restraint of trade or harm to competition. After all, both Bitcoin Cash ABC and Bitcoin Cash SV continued to trade. While the price of both may have decreased, the defendant claimed that it was not because of its alleged actions.

In early 2020, a federal judge dismissed the antitrust lawsuit without prejudice to the plaintiff filing an amended complaint containing additional allegations. The plaintiff complied, but its amended complaint was also dismissed in early 2021. The judge found that the plaintiff had again failed to prove adequately that the defendants had committed an antitrust violation.

Based on the facts of the *Bitmain* case, it is hard to see a path for plaintiffs to win these antitrust cases. If the case had progressed to discovery, perhaps the plaintiff would have found correspondence between the defendant and other individuals that unveiled plans to hijack Bitcoin Cash and make their protocol win. But it would have been difficult to conduct discovery in *Bitmain* because multiple jurisdictions would have been involved, thereby implicating various privacy laws and local government hurdles. The plaintiff would have had to establish that the defendant's conspiracy to centralize the blockchain in one protocol's favor was both anticompetitive and injurious. Antitrust law concerns itself with consumer harm or harm to competition in the industry. The only harm mentioned in the case was the value decrease of the protocols. It is hard to imagine that the court would find an unreasonable harm to the competitive marketplace from the purported conspiracy. The defendant's argument that there was no anticompetitive conduct also warrants consideration. Both sides wanted to win, so both sides increased their mining power. They were using their hashing power to expand their markets, which increased each party's mining output. In the end, the hash race to the finish was intense and vigorously fought by both parties. Is that not the essence of a competitive market?

The infamous GameStop trading fiasco in early 2021 is another example of antitrust law's application to blockchain and crypto-related technology. In *In Re: January 2021 Short Squeeze Trading Litigation*,[216] the consolidated class-action complaint alleged that multiple large hedge funds and investment firms had engaged in short selling several securities, including GameStop Corp. In addition, retail investors—regular, non-professional investors—had also invested on their own behalf, in many cases doing so en masse, hoping that the stock price would increase.

Short sellers borrow shares in stock, securities, or other assets, betting that the share price will decrease so that they can later buy the stock at a lower price and return it to the lender. The difference between the sale and the buy price is the profit. With GameStop, however, the share price *increased* as retail investors began to purchase the securities. With the stock price increasing, the defendants faced potential losses of several billion dollars in a classic "short squeeze." As the complaint explained:

> [A] short squeeze occurs when a stock or other asset rises sharply in value, distressing short positions in the asset. A short squeeze therefore is when investors in short positions are faced with a rapid increase in the shorted asset's value, exposing the short seller to increased loss. As the price of the asset rises, short sellers may face pressure to buy back shares of stock to exit their short positions to mitigate their losses. In the absence of market manipulation or some other intervention, as short sellers exit their short positions by buying shares of stock to cover their short positions, the purchase of those shares further increases the price of the stock.[217]

The plaintiffs alleged that after the close of the stock market and before the opening the next day, the defendants, including several trading platforms such as Robinhood, engaged in multiple conspiracies to preclude additional purchases of the securities. These tactics included disabling the buying features on their platforms, leaving retail investors with a quandary: sell their stock or hold on to it as prices fell. The plaintiffs also alleged that the defendants displayed loading graphics to prevent investors from purchasing more of the securities. Unable to purchase more shares, the retail investors had to sell their shares at lower prices

---

216. *In Re: January 2021 Short Squeeze Trading Litigation*, No. 21-02989-MDL-ALTONAGA/Torres, (July 27, 2021).

217. *Id.* at 36.

than they otherwise might have. The defendants' alleged goal was to drive down prices and mitigate the losses from their short positions. In so doing, they erased over $10 billion in market capitalization from the investors.

The class sought equitable relief under, among other things, Section 1 of the Sherman Act and Section 16 of the Clayton Act. In November 2021, the defendants won the first battle: The district court dismissed the plaintiffs' complaint without prejudice, finding that the plaintiffs had failed to show that there was a conspiracy between the defendants to manipulate the market. The court gave the plaintiffs until December 20, 2021, to file an amended complaint with additional allegations to fortify their claims. The amended complaint asserted various causes of action on behalf of the plaintiff and a putative class, such as negligence and gross negligence, breach of fiduciary duty, breach of implied covenants, and tortious interference with the plaintiffs' business relationships. The court declined to grant further leave to amend the complaint, as doing so would have been futile.

While the facts were complex, the core argument the plaintiffs made was simple. The proposed class alleged that they had invested money in the stock market only for the defendants to take away their ability to control their investments. The defendants allegedly prevented the market from acting freely to mitigate their losses at the plaintiffs' expense.

While the plaintiffs failed, at least temporarily (depending on the outcome of the litigation), this case serves as an example of how parties can plead conspiracy between online trading platforms and exchanges. Such internal agreements to manipulate the market occur more often in unregulated environments such as cryptocurrency exchanges than they do on the NYSE. It is unclear right now how effectively antitrust law will provide everyday investors with an avenue for redress against this type of market manipulation and anticompetitive behavior.

Little by little, blockchain technology is being construed and regulated by the legal system—from government agencies to class-action lawsuits. Claimants are making creative arguments to extend traditional statutory provisions to blockchain and crypto technology. At first, courts appeared to side with the defendants when faced with these novel issues. The biggest win to date for defendants was *Audet vs. Fraser*, where the jury held that the ICO's digital assets were not securities. As more cases are filed, courts and juries must continue to determine whether the old laws and rules apply to these novel digital technologies.

6. ARBITRATION OF DIGITAL ASSET ISSUES

Parties often choose arbitration to resolve their commercial disputes. The choice has become almost a certainty in various industries, including energy, construction, technology, aviation, financial services, and real estate. In addition, the COVID-19 pandemic has caused significant delays, budget cuts, and backlogs in domestic courts. Parties who might have otherwise filed lawsuits are turning to arbitration to settle their legal disputes.

Blockchain and cryptocurrency-related issues are likely to become more mainstream. Arbitration is therefore likely to become a common forum for these issues. In fact, arbitration may be a favorable alternative to litigation in the digital-asset arena because, as illustrated above, the current legal framework appears to be ill-equipped to settle blockchain claims. Although federal agencies have released frameworks and guidelines regarding blockchain technology and cryptocurrency, there is no consistent and reliable legislation. Judges—let alone juries—may not understand the intricacies of this evolving technology and the implicated novel legal issues. Blockchain and cryptocurrency disputes are often technical and require (or favor) panels knowledgeable in the industry.

Arbitration panels experienced in digital assets can theoretically settle these issues more quickly, at a lower cost, with more flexibility and confidentiality, and with less publicity and reputational harm than if the disputes were publicly filed in courts. One major question that remains is whether individuals can use arbitration in certain blockchain-related areas, such as smart contracts. Recall that smart contracts are self-executing contracts written in computer code, stored on the blockchain, and agreed upon by the parties in advance. As soon as the agreed-upon triggering event occurs, the contract enforces. There should be no issues of contract interpretation, breach, or even modification (unless the parties make a new smart contract). If one party believes that there is a dispute, can they resort to arbitration? Can the parties place an arbitration clause in the contract, or does the self-executing nature of these contracts render such a clause meaningless? Answers to these questions will only come with time.

Summary

The threat of private litigation to parties involved in the digital-asset marketplace not only parallels the threat from government investigations but surpasses it. Successful class actions for unregistered ICOs may require the return of all consideration plus interest to every investor. Plaintiffs can allege intellectual-property violations, antitrust violations, and state-law claims of fraud, negligence, and tort. While the future of blockchain technology is unclear, both issuers and investors must proceed with caution. It is imperative that these parties meticulously monitor new developments in the blockchain/cryptocurrency industry, including case precedent, court decisions, and the arguments and defenses made.

Issuers should further understand the risk that their ICO may be treated as an investment contract or security, which exposes them to liability absent registration or exemption. But investor protection is not a guarantee either. While investors may now feel empowered to bring class-action lawsuits against issuers for unregistered securities, they should understand that the Howey Test is malleable. For example, courts may decide that the investors' expectation of profits was unreasonable.

As litigation continues and blockchain issues are no longer novel, both parties to these transactions must understand the legal ramifications. Prudent issuers and investors will therefore need to seek experienced law firms with demonstrated knowledge in blockchain technology, cryptocurrency, and ICOs to guide them through any issues that may arise.

§ 11 Government Enforcement

For a capital market to function properly it must be fair, transparent, and organized. The Securities and Exchange Commission, or SEC, is the federal agency that enforces the federal securities laws that regulate the securities industry. Since its establishment in the 1930s, the SEC will do almost anything to expand its traditional jurisdictional basis to prevent a dysfunctional market system. Think back to the 1920s and the Great Depression. The economy and capital markets were speculative and contained false information, misleading information, and multiple instances of fraud. As soon as this bubble burst, America's economy collapsed. In May 1933, the National Bureau of Economic Research recorded an unemployment rate of about 25.6%.[218]

After this, the SEC was established, and Congress passed two bills to regulate capital markets and protect investors: (1) the U.S. Securities Act of 1933 and (2) the U.S. Exchange Act of 1934. The SEC was given jurisdiction over securities offerings (whether those securities involve stocks, bonds, notes, derivatives, investment contracts, or anything else resembling a security), the issuers of those securities, companies investing in those issued securities, brokers and dealers, and securities exchanges.[219]

The emergence of blockchain technology has created new questions for government enforcement. How does the SEC treat digital assets? From an SEC perspective, are digital assets securities? When do digital assets trigger reporting requirements? Considering crypto fraud and law-enforcement takedowns, there are many lines to be drawn between

---

218. GREG IACURCI, *Unemployment is Nearing Great Depression Levels. Here's How the Eras are Similar – and Different,* cnbc.com, (May 19, 2020).

219. 15 U.S.C. § 77b(a)(1); 15 U.S.C. § 77e; 15 U.S.C. § 80a–8; 15 U.S.C. § 78o; 15 U.S.C. § 78f.

legitimate use of new technologies and currencies and criminal enterprise.

> "Because of the volatility of the currency itself, and the difficulty in predicting how regulatory agencies will categorize cryptocurrency, any questions surrounding this medium of exchange should be addressed by experts with knowledge of current case law and regulatory decisions." Retired FBI Special Agent Marie Kondzielski

If the SEC also has jurisdiction over digital assets, what is the "securities link?" The SEC tries to answer this question in their "Framework for 'Investment Contract' Analysis of Digital Assets."[220] The framework declares that the SEC should examine digital assets to see if they have any characteristics similar to a security. If so, the SEC can and will regulate the digital asset just like a traditional security.

The SEC uses the *Howey* Test to make this determination.[221] If the SEC encounters "unique or novel instruments or arrangements" such as coins, tokens, or other digital assets, it will use this investment-contract test. Under *Howey*, if there is an investment of money in a common enterprise with a reasonable expectation of profits derived from the efforts of others, the digital asset is a security. *Howey* determines whether the SEC has jurisdiction. The *Howey* Test is explained below. The idea is that digital assets have the same economic realities as traditional securities despite the differences in form, therefore allowing the Commission to regulate them without additional congressional authorization.[222]

Assume for now that the SEC can assert jurisdiction over digital assets. What does that cover and how far does that jurisdiction extend? The SEC has jurisdiction over securities, issuers, certain companies, exchanges, and brokers and dealers. Digital-asset mining, pooled investment vehicles involving digital assets, decentralized finance, and centralized lending of digital assets may also be securities.[223] Theoretically, the SEC could extend its jurisdiction beyond securities. Consider these situations:

- Example 1: An exchange lists about 200 traditional securities and several digital assets. This is an easy case. The SEC can regulate everything on the platform based on its uncontested jurisdictional authority to regulate traditional securities.

---

220. SEC, *Framework for "Investment Contract" Analysis of Digital Assets*, seq.gov, (2019), available at https://www.sec.gov/corpfin/framework-investment-contract-analysis-digital-assets
221. *SEC v. Howey Co.*, 328 U.S. 293, (1946).
222. TODD PHILLIPS, *The SEC's Regulatory Role in the Digital Asset Markets,* americanprogress.org, (Oct. 4, 2021).
223. *Id.*

- Example 2: An exchange lists one digital asset security and fifty miscellaneous digital assets. Because the SEC can regulate the digital-asset security, it might regulate other digital assets. The SEC could still regulate these "non-securities" assets because the SEC already has its "securities link" to the exchange from the digital-asset security.
- Example 3: A broker trades and advises customers on traditional securities and digital assets. Whether these digital assets are securities or not, the SEC may likely regulate the broker's trading and investment advice for all transactions based on its jurisdictional authority to regulate brokers and dealers.
- Example 4: A broker trades and advises on one digital-asset security and several other digital assets. These other digital assets are either not securities or it is questionable whether they are securities. The SEC may regulate trades and advice of this broker because the securities link is present.

In short, if the SEC finds a securities link, everything could be subject to regulation. This is quite a malleable conclusion. It is hard to counter the SEC's goal of protecting investors and preserving capital markets when it claims to have jurisdiction over digital assets. Without congressional guidance, the exact contours of digital-asset regulation and enforcement remain murky.

1. SEC REGULATION AND THE FUTURE OF DIGITAL-ASSET SECURITIES

Assume someone buys a housing unit to live in. The housing unit is not a security.[224] But now assume that the seller offered the housing unit with a management contract that comes with specialized services for the individuals. In this latter situation, the housing unit is sold as a package—an investment-contract package—and is therefore a security.[225]

Another example is a Certificate of Deposit, or CD. CDs are not treated as a security under Section 2 of the Securities Act. But what if the CDs are sold by brokers as part of a program that offers liquidity and the possibility of profiting from interest-rate fluctuations? This CD is transformed into an investment contract—a security.[226] Any instrument or contract can be an investment contract, or security, under the right circumstances.

224. *United Hous. Found., Inc. v. Forman*, 421 U.S. 837, (1975).
225. SEC Release No. 33-5347, *Guidelines as to the Applicability of the Federal Securities Laws to Offers and Sales of Condominiums or Units in a Real Estate Development*, seq.gov, (Jan. 4, 1973).
226. *Gary Plastic Packaging Corp. v. Merrill Lynch, Pierce, Fenner & Smith, Inc.*, 756 F.2d 230, (2d Cir. 1985).

In its July 2017 DAO Report, the SEC used the *Howey* Test to find that the unregistered tokens issued by the DAO—an unincorporated organization that raised about $150 million from general solicitations to retail investors—were in fact securities despite claims that it was decentralized.[227] The SEC focused not on the technology but on the economic realities of the situation: the holders of DAO tokens expected to share in the projects' earnings as a return on their initial investments in the tokens—securities. The DAO Report produced a wave of ICO scrutiny—enforcement actions and administrative orders. For instance, the SEC's administrative order against Munchee, Inc. found that Munchee's sale of digital tokens to investors to raise funds for its food-review service (with the possibility that the value of the tokens would increase) was an unregistered securities offering that caused Munchee to stop its ICO. The SEC emphasized that this was an offering because investors could reasonably expect that Munchee's efforts could lead to an increase in the token's value and therefore generate a return on their investment.[228]

In February 2018, SEC Chairman Jay Clayton testified during a Senate hearing that "I believe every ICO I've seen is a security."[229] The SEC may be willing to work with individuals when structuring a coin or token issuance. The SEC issued a no-action letter to charter jet company, TurnKey Jet, for their plans to tokenize gift cards that would allow their customers to purchase redeemable dollar-for-dollar tokens in exchange for charter jet services or to sell the tokens to other members only.[230] At the same time, issuing more no-action letters broadens the SEC's jurisdiction, as stated by Commissioner Hester M. Peirce in May 2019.[231] At this stage, the SEC understands that it cannot stop the flourishing crypto sphere from blossoming further. The alternative is to regulate it.

Even though the SEC seeks to regulate crypto and blockchain companies with strict regulations, not every commissioner at the agency shares this position. Commissioner Hester Peirce believes that it is more productive to work with crypto firms when establishing regulations: "I

227. SEC Release No. 81207, *Report of Investigation Pursuant to Section 21(a) of the Securities Exchange Act of 1934: The DAO, Securities and Exchange Commission*, seq.gov, (July 25, 2017).
228. SEC Press Release 2017-227, *Company Halts ICO After SEC Raises Registration Concerns*, seq.gov, (Dec. 11, 2017).
229. *Virtual Currencies: The Oversight Role of the U.S. Securities and Exchange Commission and the U.S. Commodity Futures Trading Commission, U.S. Senate Committee on Banking, Housing, and Urban Affairs*, (2018), available at https://www.govinfo.gov/content/pkg/CHRG-115shrg28854/html/CHRG-115shrg28854.htm
230. SEC No-Action Letter, TurnKey Jet, Inc., (Apr. 3, 2019).
231. Speech, COMMISSIONER HESTER M. PEIRCE, "How We Howey," Securities Enforcement Forum, East Palo Alto, California, sec.gov, [Video], (May 9, 2019).

think it's safe to assume that crypto is going to grow in size... And so, what we can do now to invest in building a reasonable framework, I think, will pay off down the line."[232]

a. The SEC's Howey Test

The Howey Test is the standard the SEC uses to determine whether a digital asset is an investment contract, which requires registration with the Commission, or an exemption. It originates from a 1946 Supreme Court opinion, *SEC v. Howey, Co.*[233]

Howey involved sale-leaseback agreements of orange fields. Howey, Co. owned large tracts of citrus groves. The company sold real-estate contracts of the groves at a uniform price per acre. Howey gave the purchasers the option to lease the land back to it in a service contract for the cultivation of that land. The contract gave Howey the sole right of possession. Once the groves were harvested, Howey sold them on behalf of the owners, and the owners received an account for the harvested goods. Howey marketed the fruit through a resort hotel that it owned. The SEC brought an enforcement action against Howey for failing to register these contracts with the SEC. Ultimately, the Supreme Court determined that it was a security and set forth the standard for analyzing whether an instrument qualifies as an investment contract:

> *"[A]n investment contract for purposes of the Securities Act means a contract, transaction or scheme whereby a person* ***[1] invests his money*** *in a* ***[2] common enterprise*** *and is led to* ***[3] expect profits*** *solely from the* ***[4] efforts of the promoter or a third party*** *. . ."*[234]

It may first seem odd to say that Howey, Co. had to register its oranges as securities. But this was not a traditional enterprise. The purchasers would buy the grove and lease it back to Howey, Co. to cultivate to receive a return from the harvest. It was an investment in the same enterprise, Howey, Co., with the expectation of receiving a profit based on the cultivation efforts of Howey's personnel. From this perspective, it starts to look more like an investment contract.

While *Howey* traditionally applied to investment contracts such as shares agreements, sale leasebacks, or bond arrangements, the *Howey* Test has gained momentum for analyzing digital assets. William Hinman, Director of the SEC's Division of Corporation Finance, observed in a speech that *how* digital assets are sold can be an investment contract.

---

232. PAUL KIERNAN, *Republican SEC Commissioner Criticizes Agency's Approach to Crypto*, WALL STREET JOURNAL, (Oct. 29, 2021).
233. *SEC v. Howey Co.*, 328 U.S. 293, (1946).
234. *SEC v. Howey Co.*, 328 U.S. 293, at 327-28, (1946).

After all, the goal of the securities laws is to remove any information gaps between promoters and investors. Investors must have all relevant information to make informed investment decisions. Any promoter that does not provide this would be liable for material misstatements and lack of material disclosures. To protect investors and avoid these risks, the nation needs a regulatory framework.[235] About a year later, in April 2019, the SEC released its "Framework for 'Investment Contract' Analysis of Digital Assets,"[236] which analyzes whether a digital asset is an investment contract under *Howey's* four-pronged test:

THE *HOWEY* ELEMENTS	
The Investment of Money	Digital asset offerings and sales satisfy this prong because they are bought or acquired for value—either fiat currencies, other digital assets, or another type of consideration. Remember, value does *not* always mean cash.
Common Enterprise	This prong is also usually satisfied because the profits of digital-asset purchasers correspond to the promoter's success efforts. In fact, most ICOs state in the offering materials that they are issuing coins or tokens to pool funds for their projects' developments.
Reasonable Expectation of Profits	Profits under this prong include capital appreciation, the sharing of earnings from the use of the purchasers' funds, or the right to share in the company's income or profits. Price appreciation solely from external market conditions is not profit. For instance, if a digital asset's value increases because of inflation and this impacts the asset's supply and demand, the profit prong is not satisfied.
Reliance on the Efforts of Others	The "reliance on others" prong asks (1) whether the purchaser reasonably expects to rely on efforts of the promoter, sponsor, or other third party ("Active Participants" (APs)) and (2) whether those efforts are significant and require managerial efforts rather than more ministerial efforts. The fourth prong is more likely to be satisfied where the AP is responsible for the development, improvement, operation, promotion, or oversight of the network. If the purchasers expect the APs to carry out such duties for the digital asset to achieve its intended purpose or function, the fourth prong is satisfied.

235. Speech, WILLIAM HINMAN, *Digital Asset Transactions: When Howey Met Gary (Plastic)*, seq.gov, (Jun 14, 2018).

236. SEC, *Framework for "Investment Contract" Analysis of Digital Assets*, seq.gov, (2019), available at https://www.sec.gov/corpfin/framework-investment-contract-analysis-digital-assets

Although the SEC has turned its attention to digital assets, it has been investigating digital-asset schemes as potential securities since at least 2013. In *SEC v. Shavers et. al*, the defendants operated a Ponzi scheme where they solicited Bitcoin owners to send them their Bitcoins by promising them large returns generated through the defendants' Bitcoin arbitrage system. In their defense, the defendants argued that Bitcoin was not money and could not sustain an investment contract, but the court found that the Bitcoins were a contribution of value and constituted an investment contract. The SEC was granted summary judgment, and the court awarded $40.7 million in damages.[237] This trend of heightened SEC attention towards digital assets continues today. The future of the regulatory framework may take one of three forms: (1) *Howey* Test applies to all digital assets, (2) *Howey* Test is inapplicable to digital assets, or (3) a combination.

b. Future Scenario #1: *Howey* Test Applies to All Digital Assets

Future Scenario #1 applies the *Howey* Test to digital assets in the same way it does to traditional securities. All the SEC must do to achieve this is continue its investigative approach and progressively broaden its definition of investment contracts.

The SEC has already started to do so by noting that *Howey's* analysis depends not on the digital asset itself but on the circumstances of the offering of the digital asset. These include the marketing to investors, how it is sold at initial issuance, and whether it is resold on a secondary market—the *economic realities* of the digital asset.

For example, why would you invest in a developer's new network if there is no chance that your investment will earn a return? Since the first two elements of *Howey*—investment of money in a common enterprise—are satisfied, the SEC needs to expand their interpretation of the last two factors—expectation of profits based on the efforts of others. When grappling with an investment in digital assets, the success of the issuer's business often depends on managerial efforts of third parties. The SEC needs only point to the core purpose of the federal securities laws, which is to prevent investor misinformation. Thus, not only do issuers need to be mindful that their digital-asset issuances may be securities, but individuals with marketing, distribution, and sales responsibilities must be mindful as well. It would be hard to argue that digital assets are not securities under this future scenario.

237. *SEC v. Shavers*, 2013 U.S. Dist. LEXIS 130781, (E.D. Tex. Sept. 18, 2014).

Whether the *Howey* Test will apply to all digital assets depends on how the SEC perceives the need for regulation. This scenario may already be starting within the SEC.

First, the SEC has emphasized that digital-asset regulation is inevitable. In a public statement by SEC Chair Gary Gensler in August 2021, Gensler observed the pervasiveness of "crypto finance." People are trading tokens and lending tokens on trading platforms with over fifty to a hundred tokens listed on them. Once the SEC finds that securities link, it can regulate the entire platform. Regulation is also an unavoidable future since these platforms already implicate the federal securities laws (SEC), commodity laws (CFTC), and banking laws (Bank Secrecy Act enforced by FinCEN; Know Your Customer/Anti-Money Laundering policies).

Second, regulation prevents fraud. Unregulated foreign exchanges facilitate trading by U.S. investors through virtual private networks. These foreign exchanges are circumventing U.S. securities laws. More stringent regulation may stop these efforts, especially with cross-border issues.

Third, regulation by the SEC is the only way to protect investors. There are significant gaps in investor protection and aspects of the crypto trading and investing processes. Gensler also observed that inconsistent regulation is not "sustainable" for protecting investors, preventing illicit activity, and guaranteeing financial stability.[238]

Fourth, to promote innovation within the nation, the SEC needs to have a consistent regulatory framework for digital assets. Without this accountability and consistency, Commissioner Caroline A. Crenshaw noted in a speech in October 2021, markets cannot sustain growth, investor confidence will decline, and mass adoption cannot occur.[239] Gensler declared in his public statement that financial innovations in the nation do not thrive outside regulatory frameworks and that, to encourage crypto innovation, the nation needs regulation.[240] These examples suggest more willingness by the Commission to broaden *Howey's* application to include all digital assets and hybrids through the link analysis. And under this scenario, the *Howey* Test applies to all digital assets.

---

238. Public Statement, CHAIR GARY GENSLER, *Remarks Before the Aspen Security Forum*, seq.gov, (Aug. 3, 2021).
239. Speech, COMMISSIONER CAROLINE A. CRENSHAW, *Digital Asset Securities – Common Goals and a Bridge to Better Outcomes*, seq.gov, (Oct. 12, 2021).
240. Public Statement, CHAIR GARY GENSLER, *Remarks Before the Aspen Security Forum*, seq.gov, (Aug. 3, 2021).

There are several examples of when the SEC investigated entities and individuals for failing to register their digital assets or meet an applicable exemption. In early 2021, the SEC charged three individuals with defrauding retail investors out of over $11 million from two fraudulent and unregistered digital-asset securities offerings.[241] According to the SEC complaint, the founder of two companies and their promoter "fraudulently induced investors to buy digital-asset securities" by touting the digital-asset mining and trading platform. The SEC also alleged that the defendants promoted an unregistered ICO of B2G tokens, which contained multiple misrepresentations to investors and led to the defendants misappropriating "millions of dollars of investor funds for their own personal benefit." The DOJ filed a parallel action.

A few months later, the SEC announced that it settled charges against an ICO issuer and CEO for making "materially false and misleading statements in connection with an unregistered offer and sale of digital-asset securities."[242] The defendants had raised $7.6 million from investors through their offering of digital tokens called "LOCIcoin," which contained false statements about the company's revenues, user base, and number of employees. The SEC's order emphasized that the LOCIcoins were securities under the federal securities laws, that the defendants had not registered with the SEC, and no exemption applied. Then, in mid-September 2021, the SEC charged three media companies with conducting an illegal unregistered offering of stock and digital-asset securities called either "G-Coins" or "G-Dollars."[243] These unregistered offerings raised about $487 million from over 5,000 investors. The SEC alleged that the defendants had filed no registration statements from either offering and that the offers and sales did not qualify for a registration exemption. The defendants agreed to pay over $539 million to settle charges with the SEC.

More recently, the SEC charged BlockFi Lending, LLC (BlockFi) with failing to register the offers and sales of its retail crypto-lending product and with violating the registration provisions of the Investment Company Act of 1940.[244] BlockFi agreed to pay a $50 million penalty, cease its unregistered offers and sales of the lending product, BlockFi Interest

241. SEC Press Release 2021-22, *SEC Charges Three Individuals in Digital Asset Frauds,* seq.gov, (Feb. 1, 2021).
242. SEC Press Release 2021-108, *SEC Charges ICO Issuer and CEO With Fraud and Unregistered Securities Offering,* seq.gov, (June 22, 2021).
243. SEC Press Release 2021-175, *SEC Charges Three Media Companies with Illegal Offerings of Stock and Digital Assets,* seq.gov, (Sept. 13, 2021).
244. SEC Press Release 2022-26, *BlockFi Agrees to Pay $100 Million in Penalties and Pursue Registration of its Crypto Lending Product,* seq.gov, (Feb 14, 2022).

Accounts (BIAs), and attempt to bring its business within the provisions of the Investment Company Act within sixty days. SEC Chair Gary Gensler described it as "the first case of its kind with respect to crypto-lending platforms."[245] According to the SEC, BlockFi offered and sold BIAs to the public and, through the BIAs, the investors lent crypto assets to BlockFi in exchange for the company's promise to provide a variable monthly interest payment. The SEC concluded that the BIAs are securities, and the company needed to register its offers and sales of BIAs but failed to do so or to qualify for an exemption from SEC registration.

Consider a final example. In August 2021, the SEC announced that it had settled charges against Poloniex, LLC for operating an unregistered digital-asset exchange from July 2017 to November 2019 that allowed individuals to buy and sell digital-asset securities. Poloniex had stated around 2017 that it wanted to make new digital assets available for trading, including those that might be securities under *Howey*. The SEC determined that the digital assets made available on the company's platform were investment contracts under *Howey* and were therefore securities. The Chief of the SEC Enforcement Division's Cyber Unit asserted:

> Poloniex chose increased profits over compliance with the federal securities laws by including digital-asset securities on its unregistered exchange. . . Poloniex attempted to circumvent the SEC's regulatory regime, which applies to any marketplace for bringing together buyers and sellers of securities regardless of the applied technology.

Poloniex agreed to pay over $10 million to settle these charges.[246]

c. Future Scenario #2: *Howey* Test is Inapplicable to Digital Assets[247]

Future Scenario #2 does not apply the *Howey* Test to any digital assets. Under this approach, digital assets are distinct from traditional securities, and the investment, trading, buying, selling, and lending of digital assets are not governed by SEC regulations. Crypto and blockchain growth would stifle and produce an environment where start-ups and

245. *Id.*

246. Press Release 2021-147, *SEC Charges Poloniex for Operating Unregistered Digital Asset Exchange*, (Aug. 9, 2021).

247. This scenario only applies to a possible future where the digital assets *themselves* are not subject to SEC regulation as an investment contract or securities under the *Howey* Test. It is possible that their offering can be structured in a way that meets the definition of an investment contract, as the Supreme Court opinion, *Howey*, demonstrated with the citrus groves.

developers hesitate to launch coin/token offerings. Whether *Howey* is inapplicable to all digital assets depends on which side the SEC is closer to on the continuum between preventing fraud and permitting new projects without fear of government reprisal. It also depends on how the SEC interprets the definition of "money" for digital assets.

The SEC has taken some steps suggesting that digital assets that stand alone may not constitute securities per se. For example, Commissioner Hester M. Peirce released a Token Safe Harbor in both 2020 and 2021 to allow developers and start-ups to launch token sales without having to worry about SEC enforcement. Under her proposal, individuals and businesses would have three years to either (1) register or (2) prove that they are fully decentralized and exempt from the federal securities laws. The Safe Harbor also lists exemptions for the Exchange Act's definitions of "exchange," "broker," "dealer," and the Securities Act's registration requirements.[248]

Likewise, Representative Patrick McHenry (R-NC), ranking member on the House Financial Services Committee, released a safe-harbor bill—the Clarity for Digital Tokens Act of 2021—that mirrors Commissioner's Peirce's proposal. The bill embraces new technology and financial innovation by providing a safe harbor for digital-asset projects. Under certain conditions, the digital-asset projects are exempt from registration. Developers and start-ups can analyze whether their projects meet the definition of a security or whether the safe harbor applies to them.[249]

By exempting certain transactions, the SEC is distancing digital assets from the traditional regulatory sphere of security instruments. The SEC may also presume that digital assets are not money. For instance, even though Chair Gensler promoted digital-asset regulation in his public statement, he also distinguished digital assets from traditional fiat currencies.[250] Fiat currencies fulfil money's three purposes: unit of account, store of value, and medium of exchange. Arguably, digital assets do not. Because digital assets are speculative investments, one could classify them as an unreliable unit of account. They are not a store

248. Statement, COMMISSIONER HESTER M. PEIRCE, *Token Safe Harbor Proposal 2.0 (April 13, 2021);* GitHub, *Commissioner Peirce, Safe Harbor 2.0.,* 2021.

249. Press Release, PATRICK MCHENRY Ranking Republican, *McHenry Introduces Legislation to Provide Legal Clarity & Certainty for Digital Asset Projects: New Bill Provides a "Safe Harbor" for Digital Token Innovation,* Financial Services Republicans, republicans-financialservices.house.gov (Oct. 5, 2021); NIKHILESH DE, *U.S. Lawmaker Proposes Safe Harbor Bill, Echoing SEC Commissioner Peirce*, coindesk.com, (Oct. 5, 2021).

250. Public Statement, CHAIR GARY GENSLER, *Remarks Before the Aspen Security Forum,* seq.gov, (Aug. 3, 2021).

of value because their value is both speculative and volatile. They are rarely a medium of exchange.

Purchasing digital assets looks a lot like betting on the success of the company—a gamble.[251] These circumstances are not purchases or value exchanges of an asset in exchange for goods or services. Applying the federal securities laws to digital assets just like traditional security instruments does not make sense. Regulation would lead to more questions, uncertainty, and fear of SEC enforcement by developers and start-ups when using blockchain technology and cryptos. In this scenario, digital assets are not securities, and there is no need to apply the *Howey* Test.

d. Future Scenario #3: Hybrid

A hybrid scenario is conceivable. Like other controversial classifications (for example, what constitutes hate speech or second-amendment issues), courts may be inclined to draw the line between securities and non-securities on a case-by-case basis.

This combination can take one of two forms: first, situations in which the *Howey* Test applies to some digital assets and not to others (Commingled Loss) and second, situations in which issuers offer digital assets as a security but the digital asset is then sold as something other than a security (Transformative Loss). To understand the first form, recall the difference between a security token and a utility token. A security token is an equity or investment token on the blockchain. Think of security tokens as cryptographic securities offerings. They do not grant individuals access to a certain ecosystem but give individuals a share in the company. These crypto shares can return a profit based on the success of the company.

Utility tokens are tokens that give individuals a utility within a certain ecosystem also on the blockchain. They do not provide individuals with a share or interest in the company's profits and are not created as an investment opportunity. Individuals can use these tokens on the platform for specific services. Most ICOs issue utility tokens to help companies raise money in their projects. This scenario applies the *Howey* Test to security tokens and exempt utility tokens. Because this test is a mix of applying *Howey* to some tokens and not others, it is similar to where we are today. To an extent, the issue is not whether the government can regulate one token over the other. The issue is whether a particular coin or token is more like a security token or a utility token and where to draw this line. The first form of this future would have meticulous guidelines

251. Speech, WILLIAM HINMAN, *Digital Asset Transactions: When Howey Met Gary (Plastic)*, seq.gov, (Jun 14, 2018).

for making this distinction and would apply the federal securities laws for issuances that are clear instances of security tokens and exempt issuances utility tokens.

The second instance involves situations in which the digital asset started as a security offering but then transformed into something that no longer qualifies as a security offering under current securities definitions. This was the subject of a speech by William Hinman, Director of the Division of Corporation Finance, in June 2018.[252] Transformative loss involves tokens that no longer have a central enterprise to invest in or tokens that individuals use only on the created network after issuance. The network has become decentralized enough that the individuals no longer expect a third party to carry out managerial duties. Consider a few simplified examples:

- Take Bitcoin as our first example. Bitcoin doesn't entail any central third-party control or managerial efforts. Its network is decentralized. There is therefore no need to apply the federal securities laws' disclosure provisions to Bitcoin since there are no investor-information gaps.
- Now consider a token—any token—issued to the public but whose network depends on the operations of central actors for the enterprise to succeed. Investor gaps are possible here since other individuals are controlling the entire investment operation. Applying the federal securities laws to this instance makes sense. If these third parties make material misstatements or engage in fraud to encourage investment, the securities laws will protect those investors.
- Lastly, consider a token on a decentralized network that is a clear instance of a utility token, requiring no registration for the token itself. Assume now that the issuer structures its offering package with other benefits. The issuer places the token in a fund and sells interests, which allows for the individuals' profits to grow based on the issuer's efforts. This investment package is now an investment contract—a security—that had to comply with the federal securities laws. A useful question to consider here is "would the investor benefit from the securities laws' mandatory investment and risks disclosures for this particular project?"

Considering the above future scenarios—and available forms—one can see that each scenario is possible. The SEC is taking steps down each road but has not yet released guidance to draw any clear lines between these possibilities.

252. Speech, WILLIAM HINMAN, *Digital Asset Transactions: When Howey Met Gary (Plastic)*, seq.gov, (Jun 14, 2018).

2. THE TAX IMPLICATIONS OF DIGITAL ASSETS AND IRS PROSECUTION

Like SEC jurisdiction over digital assets, the IRS's jurisdiction in this area is unsettled. And like the SEC, the IRS is eager to expand its authority over the cryptocurrency transactions of U.S. taxpayers. But crypto transactions do not always occur within the United States. In fact, many do not. Foreign crypto exchanges tend to be more accessible and less regulated. And although some foreign exchanges ban U.S. citizens from creating accounts, determined users can bypass these bans by using virtual private networks (VPNs) to conceal their true location. Although these transactions involve multiple countries and foreign jurisdictions, the government does not require a tax treaty or other treaty to go after the foreign assets of U.S. taxpayers.

- Example: Suppose Charles, a U.S. taxpayer, has engaged in cryptocurrency transactions worth over $30,000 over the past five years on Krypt-EX—a foreign cryptocurrency exchange. Charles does not report any gains, trades, or exchanges to the IRS. The IRS has reason to believe that there is underreporting of crypto transactions from U.S. taxpayers using Krypt-EX. Can the IRS obtain details on Krypt-EX account users and their transactions? The answer here is likely *yes*. The IRS already has many tools to achieve this. For instance, if it has sufficient information that Charles is evading taxes, it can issue a subpoena to Charles directly. If it suspects that Krypt-EX is facilitating crypto trading by U.S. individuals and those individuals are not reporting such trades, the IRS can issue a broad third-party document request to Krypt-EX demanding account details on U.S. individuals who engaged in trades over $20,000 in the past five years. This will include Charles.

Foreign companies are outside U.S. subpoena powers. In practice, U.S. law-enforcement agencies may rely on existing or newly enacted bi- or multilateral legal assistance cooperation treaties.[253] Law enforcement might also have leverage over the foreign company when the foreign company has a U.S. subsidiary or business operations in the United States.

a. The IRS's Position on New Technologies

The IRS first started releasing guidance on digital assets—or, as the IRS calls them, "virtual currencies"—in 2014 with its IRS Notice 2014-

253. *United States and Switzerland Agree on Access to Swiss Bank Information,* 103 AMERICAN JOURNAL OF INTERNATIONAL LAW 4, 748-750, (Feb. 27, 2017).

21.[254] This Notice defines virtual currency as "a digital representation of value that functions as a medium of exchange, a unit of account, and/or a store of value." The IRS clarifies that virtual currencies will be treated as property for federal income-tax purposes. The boom of virtual currencies in the following years prompted further action. Realizing that too few taxpayers reported their virtual currencies as property, the IRS sent a reminder to taxpayers in 2018 to disclose these transactions or be subject to penalties, interest, IRS audits, or even criminal scrutiny.[255]

IRS 2018 WARNING LETTER

The Internal Revenue Service today reminded taxpayers that income from virtual currency transactions is reportable on their income tax returns.

Virtual-currency transactions are taxable by law just like transactions in any other property. The IRS has issued guidance in IRS Notice 2014-21 for use by taxpayers and their return preparers that addresses transactions in virtual currency, also known as digital currency.

Taxpayers who do not properly report the income-tax consequences of virtual-currency transactions can be audited for those transactions and, when appropriate, can be liable for penalties and interest.

In more extreme situations, taxpayers could be subject to criminal prosecution for failing to properly report the income-tax consequences of virtual-currency transactions. Criminal charges could include tax evasion and filing a false tax return. Anyone convicted of tax evasion is subject to a prison term of up to five years and a fine of up to $250,000. Anyone convicted of filing a false return is subject to a prison term of up to three years and a fine of up to $250,000. . .[256]

Even this notification did not seem to be enough. In July 2019, the IRS sent out over 10,000 letters to taxpayers who had either failed to report their virtual-currency transactions or who did not report them accurately.[257] These letters demanded that taxpayers file amended returns and pay back taxes.[258] The IRS issued them as a direct result of the information the IRS had gained from cryptocurrency exchange, Coinbase—that was obligated by court order in 2018 to turn over transaction data for over 13,000 users.[259]

254. IRS Notice 2014-21.
255. IR-2018-71, *IRS Reminds Taxpayers to Report Virtual Currency Transactions,* (March 23, 2018).
256. IR-2018-71, *IRS Reminds Taxpayers to Report Virtual Currency Transactions,* (March 23, 2018).
257. IRS News Release IR-2019-132, *IRS Has Begun Sending Letters to Virtual Currency Owners Advising Them to Pay Back Taxes, File Amended Returns; Part of Agency's Larger Efforts,* irs.gov, (Jul. 26, 2019).
258. IRS Letters 6173; 6174; 6174-A.
259. KELLY PHILLIPS ERB, *Coinbase Notifies Customers That It Will Turn Over Court-Ordered Data,* forbes.com, (Feb. 8, 2018).

COINBASE ORDER
Coinbase is ORDERED to produce these documents for accounts with at least the equivalent of $20,000 in any one transaction type (buy, sell, send, or receive) in any one year during the 2013 to 2015 period: • the taxpayer ID number, • name, • birth date, • address, • records of account activity including transaction logs or other records identifying the date, amount, and type of transaction (purchase/sale/exchange), the post transaction balance, and the names of counterparties to the transaction, and • all periodic statements of account or invoices (or the equivalent).[260]

Starting with tax year 2019, the IRS also added a new question to Form 1040:

> *"At any time during [the taxable year], did you receive, sell, send, exchange or otherwise acquire any financial interest in any virtual currency?"*[261]

It took the IRS five years to go from simple guidance to mandatory crypto disclosures. And that's where the country stands today.

Despite the IRS's position that Bitcoin is property, several district courts have held that Bitcoin is money under various federal statutes. In *United States v. Ulbricht*, the district court rejected the defendant's argument that he could not be liable for money laundering because he used Bitcoin and thus engaged in no financial transaction under the statute. In holding that Bitcoins are funds, the district judge noted:

> Bitcoins carry value—that is their purpose and function—and act as a medium of exchange. Bitcoins may be exchanged for legal tender, be it U.S. dollars, Euros, or some other currency. . . Put simply, "funds" can be used to pay for things in the colloquial sense. Bitcoins can be either used directly to pay for certain things or can act as a medium of exchange and be converted into a currency which can pay for things. . . The money laundering statute is broad enough to encompass use of bitcoins in financial transactions.[262]

Also important was that the judge distanced Bitcoin from common perceptions of illegality, money laundering, and Silk-Road associations:

260. *United States v. Coinbase, Inc.*, Order RE Petition to Enforce IRS Summons, No.17-CV-01431-JSC, (N.D. Cal. Nov. 28, 2017).
261. IRS 2019 Form 1040.
262. *United States v. Ulbricht*, 31 F. Supp. 3d 540, 548, 570, (S.D.N.Y. 2014).

> [A]n allegation that bitcoins are used as a payment system is insufficient in and of itself to state a claim for money laundering. The fact that bitcoins allow for anonymous transactions does not ipso facto mean that those transactions relate to unlawful activities. The anonymity by itself is not a crime.[263]

Thus, using bitcoins is not a crime by itself, which was important to make clear in 2013 during the Silk Road's operation and closure. Former DOJ Trial Attorney John Sellers explained that the court in *Ulbricht* did not find that Bitcoin was a "monetary instrument" under 18 U.S.C. 1956; rather, the Court seems to have more reasonably determined that the Bitcoin transactions at issue constituted "financial transactions" under the statute because they represented the movement of "funds."

Consider another example. In *United States v. Murgio*, one of the defendant's arguments was that Bitcoin is not funds and therefore not currency. He held that the government's allegation that the Bitcoin exchange he ran was an unlicensed money-transmitting business in violation of federal law had to fail.[264] The district judge rejected this premise and noted:

> "[F]unds," for the purposes of §1960, means pecuniary resources, which are generally accepted as a medium of exchange or a means of payment. Applying that definition here, bitcoins are funds within the plain meaning of that term. Bitcoins can be accepted "as a payment for goods and services" or bought "directly from an exchange with [a] bank account." They therefore function as "pecuniary resources" and are "used as a medium of exchange" and "a means of payment."[265]

A few years later in *United States v. Harmon*, the Chief Judge wrote that:

> [M]oney, as detailed below, commonly means a medium of exchange, method of payment, or store of value. Bitcoin is these things... Bitcoin can be used to pay for goods or services. . . Bitcoin can also be exchanged for conventional currency... In addition, Bitcoin is viewed by many as holding value.[266]

In these two instances, classifying Bitcoin as money was critical to the courts' decisions to not dismiss charges and proceed against the defendants under the applicable federal statutes. Courts that have disagreed with this characterization have had their holdings overturned by subsequent congressional legislation. In *Florida v. Espinoza*, the

---

263. *United States v. Ulbricht*, 31 F. Supp. 3d 540, 569, (S.D.N.Y. 2014).
264. *United States v. Murgio*, 209 F. Supp. 3d 698, (S.D.N.Y. 2016).
265. *Id.* at 707.
266. *United States v. Harmon*, 474 F. Supp. 3d 76, 87, 89, (D.D.C. 2020).

Florida court dismissed money-laundering charges for the defendant's sale of Bitcoin to undercover law-enforcement officers because it held that Bitcoin is not money.[267] The Florida legislature amended the Florida Money Laundering Act, and Florida's governor signed a bill to broaden the definition of "monetary instrument" to include "virtual currency"—"a medium of exchange in electronic or digital format that is not a coin or currency of the United States or any other country."[268]

b. Reporting my Cryptocurrency Gains/Losses

So how does one report cryptocurrency gains and losses? What is a taxable crypto event? Are crypto gains ordinary or capital income? Can you take a deduction for crypto business activities? Let's break these questions down into three sub-topics: (1) taxable crypto events, (2) crypto-mining activities, and (3) the reporting process.

Taxable Crypto Events

Virtual-currency transactions are taxable events that can be either ordinary or capital income. Examples of taxable crypto events include receiving, selling, sending, exchanging, or acquiring virtual currencies, selling or receiving air drops, mining coins, employment income in the form of virtual currencies, or income from ICOs.

Crypto-Mining Activities

Mining deserves its own section because it is subject to two taxable events. The first tax event occurs when the taxpayer mines the cryptocurrency and receives new cryptocurrency as a reward. The second tax event occurs when the taxpayer disposes of their new cryptocurrency. The former is ordinary income, while the latter is capital gains/losses. Taxpayers may also be subject to self-employment tax because of their mining activities. Businesses that mine virtual currencies may have several deductions available for operating a mining business under Section 162 of the I.R.C.[269]—including electricity, repairs, rental unit, and mining equipment. Taxpayers may also offset mining losses against other income.

Let's consider an example of crypto mining:

- Example: Assume Janet earns 0.5 bitcoin from her mining activities. At the time, Bitcoin's FMV is $40,000. Janet has a realized income of $20,000. This is her ordinary income. She takes a cost basis of $20,000 in the mined virtual currency. Janet holds on to her Bitcoin for two years and then decides to sell. At the end of the second year, the value of Bitcoin is $60,000. Her investment is now worth $30,000. When she sells, she realizes a long-term

267. Order Granting Motion to Dismiss, *Florida v. Espinoza*, (July 22, 2016).
268. Fla. Stat. § 896.101(2)(j).
269. 26 U.S. Code § 162 – Trade or Business Expenses.

capital gain of $10,000 ($30,000 FMV at time of disposition minus her $10,000 cost basis). Because this is a long-term capital gain, the IRS will tax it at Janet's preferential capital gains tax rate.

Despite existing tax provisions, there is still uncertainty on reporting mining activities, as well as a significant lack of clarity on whether mining companies or staking companies should be treated as brokers. U.S. Senators Ron Wyden of Oregon and Cynthia Lummis of Wyoming introduced legislation to amend the definition of digital asset "broker" within the Infrastructure Investment and Jobs Act/Bipartisan Infrastructure Framework (H.R. 3684) signed into law by President Biden.[270] The current legal definition of broker includes various crypto entities, such as mining or staking companies, and requires them to comply with certain IRS reporting requirements. The amendment made by these senators clarifies that the definition of broker would exclude miners, stakers, wallet providers and developers, as well as ensuring that only individuals and entities with access to material information must report to the IRS. Senator Wyden explained:

> With the infrastructure bill on the verge of becoming law, it's critically important to protect innovation in the digital asset space . . . Our bill makes clear that the new reporting requirements do not apply to individuals developing blockchain technology and wallets. This will protect American innovation while at the same time ensuring those who buy and sell cryptocurrency pay the taxes they already owe.[271]

Senator Lummis added, "I'm proud to introduce this bipartisan bill to ensure that our tax system reflects the realities of digital assets and distributed-ledger technology." Senator Ted Cruz of Texas has been an outspoken critic of the current definition and an advocate for amendment. When arguing against new tax requirements for crypto-mining businesses within the new infrastructure bill, Senator Cruz stated the following:

> [I]f the underlying language in this bill goes into effect, it will have devastating effects . . . The current bill widens the definition of broker, those who would have to collect information on cryptocurrency consumers and report this information to the IRS. It would force every single participant in the cryptocurrency structure to operate as

---

270. H.R.3684 – Infrastructure Investment and Jobs Act, 117th Congress (2021-2022), congress.gov (last visited Apr. 22, 2022),aAvailable at https://www.congress.gov/bill/117th-congress/house-bill/3684/text?__cf_chl_jschl_tk__=5x7ZkaJ_1DMIpVTg5Y_yDrdiVSyAC.bHPBO8SiOaP9k 1636402295-0-gaNycGzNDSU.
271. CYNTHIA LUMMIS, Senator for Wyoming, *Wyden & Lummis introduce Bill to Fix Broker Definition for Digital Assets,* lummis.senate.gov, (Nov. 15, 2021).

a financial institution, which would mean they would have to provide consumer information to the IRS, even if they don't have access to that information. This overly broad definition of the word "broker" will block rapid innovation in cryptocurrencies and it will endanger the privacy of many Americans and cryptocurrencies. This is wrong.[272]

The Reporting Process

Taxpayers must report cryptocurrency gains, losses, exchanges, and dispositions on their tax returns. They use Form 8949 and Form 1040 Schedule B, Schedule C, and Schedule D to report these events. Below is a succinct step-by-step guide to the crypto reporting process.

- *Determine whether you engaged in virtual-currency transactions.* Taxpayers must disclose to the IRS whether they engaged in virtual-currency transactions. Answering no to this question when the answer is yes may lead to federal criminal prosecution if the IRS opens an investigation.
- *Determine whether your virtual-currency transactions are ordinary or capital.* This question is important because different tax rates may apply. The difference depends on the nature, holding period, and purpose of the transaction. Capital gains or capital losses result from the following: virtual-currency dispositions, trades, and exchanges that taxpayers hold for over one year; exchanging digital tokens or selling air drops. Ordinary income includes the following: digital-currency dispositions, trades, and exchanges that taxpayers hold for one year or less, mining coins from a mining business, ICOs, employment income in the form of cryptocurrency, or receiving air drops.
- *Determine your virtual-currency capital gains and losses.* Holding periods of one year or less produce short-term capital gains or losses, while holding periods of over one-year produce long-term capital gains or losses. Taxpayers then net these transactions. The IRS taxes short-term gains at ordinary income rates (as high as 37% for tax year 2020) and long-term gains at preferential rates (either 0%, 15%, or 20%, depending on income). Capital losses can offset capital gains on other assets and up to $3,000 of ordinary income.
- *Complete IRS Form 8949, Sales, and other Dispositions of Capital Assets.* While traditionally used for stocks and bonds, taxpayers use this form for virtual currency sales and dispositions—virtual-currency capital gains/losses and holding periods.

272. Press Release, Ted Cruz, U.S. Senator for Texas, *Sen. Cruz Leads Fight to Remove Harmful Regulations on Cryptocurrency from Wasteful Infrastructure Bill,* cruz.senate.gov, (Aug. 9, 2021).

- *Transfer the net amount on Form 8949 to Schedule D.* Taxpayers must also report their capital gains and losses from all sources on Schedule D.
- *Calculate any cryptocurrency ordinary income.* Taxpayers must then report their virtual-currency transactions that constitute ordinary income. Taxpayers need different forms for different purposes: (1) taxpayers use Schedule 1 for reporting virtual-currency income from hobbies and income from airdrops, forks, and wages, (2) Schedule B for reporting virtual-currency staking interest earned, and (3) Schedule C for reporting virtual-currency income earned from operating a business.
- *Complete the remaining sections of the tax return.* Once complete, your tax return is ready for the year.

3. CRYPTOCURRENCY-RELATED CRIMES AND TAX EVASION

There are several statutes being used by the IRS to prosecute crimes related to digital assets or cryptocurrency. For example, the IRS investigates tax evasion and money laundering. In the United States, money laundering is criminalized under the Money Laundering Control Act, contained in § 1956 and 1957 of Title 18 of the U.S. Code.

MONEY LAUNDERING
18 U.S.C. Section 1956 criminalizes the transportation or transmission of funds (1) with the intent to promote the unlawful activity, or (2) knowing that the funds represent the proceeds of a specified unlawful activity and that its transportation or transmission is designed to conceal the true source of the proceeds. Section 1957 makes it a crime to engage in a financial transaction in criminally derived property with a value greater than $10,000 and that stems from a specified unlawful activity.[273]

The IRS estimates that tax evasion in the United States totals over $1 trillion a year—an estimate higher than the year before because it now includes tax evasion through cryptocurrencies.[274]

The Bank Secrecy Act outlines various regulations and policies to combat money laundering, such as strengthening AML/KYC policies and filing reports of suspicious activity. 18 U.S.C. § 1343 criminalizes wire fraud.

---

273. 18 U.S.C. § 1957.

274. LAURA DAVISON & BLOOMBERG, *The IRS says it has a $1 trillion tax cheat problem,* fortune.com, (Apr. 13, 2021).

WIRE FRAUD
Whoever, having devised or intending to devise any scheme or artifice to defraud, or for obtaining money or property by means of false or fraudulent pretenses, representations, or promises, transmits or causes to be transmitted by means of wire, radio, or television communication in interstate or foreign commerce, any writings, signs, signals, pictures, or sounds for the purpose of executing such scheme or artifice, shall be fined under this title or imprisoned not more than twenty years, or both.[275]

Thus, if someone commits a fraud by using a form of wire communication such as a phone, email, picture, sounds, or instant message, wire fraud applies.

Along with wire fraud, 18 U.S.C. § 1341 also criminalizes mail fraud.[276] This statute broadly prohibits any fraudulent scheme that uses the Postal Service or any private or commercial interstate carrier. It provides more coverage for schemes that avoid using the electronic means of communication covered by the wire-fraud statute.

MAIL FRAUD
Whoever, having devised or intending to devise any scheme or artifice to defraud, or for obtaining money or property by means of false or fraudulent pretenses, representations, or promises, or to sell, dispose of, loan, exchange, alter, give away, distribute, supply, or furnish or procure for unlawful use any counterfeit or spurious coin, obligation, security, or other article, or anything represented to be or intimated or held out to be such counterfeit or spurious article, for the purpose of executing such scheme or artifice or attempting so to do, places in any post office or authorized depository for mail matter, any matter or thing to be sent or delivered by the Postal Service, or deposits or causes to be deposited any matter or thing to be sent or delivered by any private or commercial interstate carrier, or takes or receives therefrom, any such matter or thing, or knowingly causes to be delivered by mail or such carrier according to the direction thereon, or at the place at which it is directed to be delivered by the person to whom it is addressed, any such matter or thing, shall be fined under this title or imprisoned not more than twenty years, or both.[277]

If either the wire- or mail-fraud crimes involve a financial institution, the individual "shall be fined not more than $1,000,000 or imprisoned not more than thirty years, or both."[278] The IRS and DOJ have used these statutes and others to prosecute crimes involving cryptocurrency or digital-asset transactions. For example, on March 24, 2022, the DOJ charged two defendants with conspiracy to commit wire fraud and conspiracy to commit money laundering in connection with a million-dollar scheme to

275. 18 U.S.C. § 1343.
276. 18 U.S.C. § 1341.
277. 18 U.S.C. § 1341.
278. *Id.*; 18 U.S.C. § 1343.

defraud purchasers of NFTs advertised as "Frosties."[279] According to the DOJ, Frosties purchasers were told they would be eligible for rewards, such as giveaways, early access to a metaverse game, and exclusive mint passes to upcoming Frosties seasons. The DOJ alleged that the defendants abruptly abandoned the project within hours of selling out of Frosties NFTs, deactivated the Frosties website, and transferred around $1.1 million in cryptocurrency proceeds they earned from selling the NFTs to cryptocurrency wallets under their control.

a. The Government's Ploy to Use Private Companies

U.S. taxpayers are increasingly circumventing bans meant to stop them from accessing overseas crypto exchanges such as FTX and Binance by using VPNs.

COURT ORDER AUTHORIZING JOHN DOE SUMMONS TO KRAKEN

User Identity Information

1. Account user registration records for each account owned or controlled by the User including:
    a. User profile, User preferences, or account application information, regardless of how it is labelled or maintained, as follows:
        i. Name (including full name, any pseudonym, or any user ID);
        ii. Date of Birth;
        iii. Taxpayer Identification Number;
        iv. Physical Address;
        v. Telephone Number;
        vi. Email Address;
    b. History of all changes to the personal information identified above since the inception of the account;
    c. Complete User history for internal protocol addresses used to access the account; and
    d. Complete User payment methods (e.g., linked bank or credit card accounts) regardless of date.

This request does not include passwords, pins, private keys, security settings, and account recovery information.[280]

VPNs can hide a user's location, thereby allowing U.S. users to access these non-U.S. exchanges and bypass identity checks—especially those that aim to filter out American citizens.[281] The IRS has responded by issuing what is called a "John Doe summons" to crypto exchanges and going after these exchanges in the federal court. A John Doe summons demands that the company release requested information to the IRS.

279. DOJ Press Release 22-087, *Two Defendants Charged in Non-Fungible Token ("NFT") Fraud and Money Laundering Scheme,* justice.gov, (Mar. 24, 2022).

280. *Court Authorizes Service of John Doe Summons Seeking Identities of U.S. Taxpayers Who Have Used Cryptocurrency*, Kraken, Case 3:21-CV-02201-JCS, (April 14, 2021).

281. ALEXANDER OSIPOVICH, *U.S. Crypto Traders Evade Offshore Exchange Bans,* THE WALL STREET JOURNAL, (2021).

In early 2021, crypto companies Kraken[282] and Circle Internet Financial, Inc. (including Poloniex, LLC)[283] received John Doe summonses from the IRS. These summonses required the exchanges to turn over user account details from 2016 to 2020 with at least $20,000 in transaction value over that period.[284] The IRS believes that issuing John Doe summonses will encourage non-compliant crypto traders to come forward voluntarily. The IRS might send another round of IRS letters to taxpayers under investigation, just as it did with Coinbase. Coinbase received a John Doe summons in 2016, litigated the case for a while, and finally complied with the court order in 2018.[285] U.S. Commissioner of the Internal Revenue, Chuck Rettig, hopes that these John Doe summonses will help the IRS uncover instances where taxpayers failed to report their virtual-currency transactions.[286]

Under Section 7609(f) of the Internal Revenue Code, a John Doe summons must (1) relate to the investigation of a group of persons, (2) contain a reasonable basis for believing that the group violated tax laws, and (3) the information sought is not readily available from other sources.[287]

The Taxpayer First Act of 2019 added another procedural burden to these summonses, requiring that they be "narrowly tailored to information that pertains to the failure (or potential failure) of the person or group or class of persons" to comply with U.S. tax laws. John Doe summonses are supposed to seek information about an individual requested by the IRS. Instead, these summonses are more like a hunt for an unknown number/group of individuals that fall under a broad description of "users who engaged in X number of virtual-currency transactions for X number of years." A John Doe summons is used to get names and details on individuals from financial institutions.[288]

---

282. DOJ Press Release 21-410, *Court Authorizes Service of John Doe Summons Seeking Identities of U.S. Taxpayers Who Have Used Cryptocurrency,* justice.gov, (May 5, 2021).
283. DOJ Press Release 21-298, *Court Authorizes Service of John Doe Summons Seeking Identities of U.S. Taxpayers Who Have Used Cryptocurrency,* justice.gov, (Apr. 1, 2021).
284. SHEHAN CHANDRASEKERA, *IRS Is Catching Crypto Tax Cheats Via John Doe Summons,* forbes.com, (Apr. 2, 2021).
285. KELLY PHILLIPS ERB, *Coinbase Notifies Customers That It Will Turn Over Court-Ordered Data,* forbes.com, (Feb. 8, 2018).
286. ROBERT W. WOOD, *More IRS Summonses for Crypto Exchange Account Holder,* Cointelegraph.com, (Apr. 18, 2021).
287. I.R.C. § 7609(f).
288. ROBERT W. WOOD, *More IRS Summonses for Crypto Exchange Account Holder,* cointelegraph.com, (Apr. 18, 2021).

Before 2008, Swiss banking was secret and untouchable. Considering that Swiss law prohibits banks from divulging account holder identities, how did the U.S. government get the information of U.S. taxpayers from Swiss accounts? With John Doe summonses, threats of prosecution, and political pressure. These summonses enable the IRS to gather the names and amounts of transaction values for cryptocurrency exchanges. Courts grant the IRS latitude in requesting these summonses to gather information potentially relevant to virtual-currency transactions.[289]

This raises serious privacy issues, as users of these exchanges may not know that the federal government is obtaining their information—whether it is shared by cryptocurrency exchanges or gathered from Facebook posts that could corroborate tax-fraud allegations. Privacy laws do not apply to social-media content, so the IRS can check user information on any social media site, whether it's Facebook, Instagram, or Twitter.[290]

- Example: Assume Peter posts on Facebook: "I bought a bunch of Shiba Inu tokens a few months ago and now sold them for $5,000 on Krypt-ME! #good foreign exchange companies for quick & easy conversion." If Peter does not report this gain to the IRS, the IRS has a case of tax evasion against Peter, or at least an investigative starting point. The post also mentions the name of the foreign-exchange company that allegedly facilitates "quick and easy" transfers, which is another way to say, "less user-identity verifications and a quick setup." With that, the IRS has a basis to issue a third-party summons to Krypt-ME to see if there are U.S. taxpayers failing to report their crypto income. It can also follow the hashtag to investigate other foreign exchanges that do the same.

The investigative avenues are almost endless.

b. Future of IRS Enforcement

The United States can expect more IRS enforcement cases for instances of tax evasion or false reporting of virtual-currency transactions. The IRS Office of Fraud Enforcement released its "Operation Hidden Treasure" in March 2021. This is a dedicated group of agents trained in virtual-currency tracking focused on taxpayers who omit crypto income

289. DASHIELL C. SHAPIRO, *Cryptocurrency and the Shifting IRS Enforcement Model,* STANFORD JOURNAL OF BLOCKCHAIN LAW & POLICY (2018).
290. BECKY KRAMER, *WSU Professor Says IRS is Breaking Privacy Laws by Mining Social Media,* spokesman.com, (Aug. 25, 2017).

from their tax returns.[291] And to help it coordinate with other federal agencies, the IRS has created a specialized task force within its Criminal Investigation Division to investigate and prosecute tax evasion from the failure to report or false reporting of virtual-currency transactions.

The United States can expect more John Doe summonses towards both domestic and foreign cryptocurrency exchanges. Issuing John Doe summonses to banks was not the only reason for uncovering Swiss bank accounts from 2008 to 2009. The IRS also issued theses summonses to couriers such as FedEx, DHL, and UPS to see which Americans were communicating with foreign banks. The IRS will likely continue to use private companies to their advantage when attempting to uncover hidden crypto income. Courier services will not always have the desired information in cases involving social media. Companies such as Facebook, Twitter, Google, and other tech giants, as well as Internet Service Providers (ISPs), will be valuable sources of information to the IRS.[292]

4. THE FTC AND BLOCKCHAIN TECHNOLOGY

The Federal Trade Commission (FTC) is the U.S. federal agency responsible for protecting consumers and promoting competition. The agency seems more accepting of cryptocurrencies as a popular method of payment and store of value:

> Consumers today have ever greater options to store, share, and spend money with the aid of new technologies entering the market at breakneck speed. These emerging financial technologies can empower consumers by providing greater financial choices and unprecedented convenience. At the same time, market participants offering these exciting new products must keep in mind important consumer protection principles as they continue to innovate for consumers' benefit.[293]

The agency has also been both active and vocal when it comes to blockchain regulation and cryptocurrencies. In late 2014, the FTC published a business blog explaining Bitcoin in detail to consumers,[294]

291. GUINEVERE MOORE, *Operation Hidden Treasure Is Here. If You Have Unreported Crypto, Get Legal Advice,* forbes.com, (Mar. 6, 2021).
292. DASHIELL C. SHAPIRO, *Cryptocurrency and the Shifting IRS Enforcement Model,* STANFORD JOURNAL OF BLOCKCHAIN LAW & POLICY (2018).
293. FTC, *Financial Technology: Protecting Consumers on the Cutting Edge of Financial Transactions*, available at https://www.ftc.gov/news-events/topics/consumer-finance/financial-technology
294. NICOLE V. FLEMING, *A Bitcoin Breakdown*, ftc.gov, (Sept. 23, 2014).

and in 2015, another blog about the risks of using cryptocurrencies as a payment method and what customers should know "[b]efore paying with bitcoins..."[295] Further, in early 2018, the FTC published a business blog urging consumers to "[k]now the risks before investing in cryptocurrencies," cautioning the following:

- Cryptocurrencies aren't backed by a government or central bank.
- If you store your cryptocurrency online, you don't have the same protections as a bank account.
- A cryptocurrency's value can change constantly.
- Nothing about cryptocurrencies makes them a fool-proof investment.
- No one can guarantee you'll make money off your investment.
- Not all cryptocurrencies or the companies behind them are the same.[296]

That said, the FTC has wasted no time initiating investigations and filing complaints for alleged cryptocurrency scams and harmful schemes involving blockchain technology. In early 2016, the FTC settled charges against operators of a Bitcoin-mining operation for allegedly deceiving customers. The FTC's complaint alleged that the defendants "charged consumers thousands of dollars for its Bitcoin-mining machines, but then failed to deliver the computers until they were practically useless, or in many cases, did not provide the computers at all."[297] The Director of the FTC's Bureau of Consumer Protection made clear that "[e]ven in the fast-moving world of virtual currencies like Bitcoin, companies can't deceive people about their products."[298]

About two years later in another FTC investigation, the FTC persuaded a federal court to enjoin four individuals from allegedly engaging in "deceptive money-making schemes involving cryptocurrencies."[299] The defendants' schemes—known as Bitcoin Funding and My7Network—"falsely promised that participants could earn large returns by paying cryptocurrency such as Bitcoin or Litecoin to enroll in the schemes." The

295. KRISTIN COHEN, *Before Paying with Bitcoins...*, ftc.gov, (June 22, 2015).
296. ELIZABETH KWOK, *Know the Risks Before Investing in Cryptocurrencies*, ftc.gov, (Feb. 16, 2018).
297. FTC Press Release, *Operators of Bitcoin Mining Operation Butterfly Labs Agree to Settle FTC Charges They Deceived Consumers*, ftc.gov, (Feb. 18, 2016).
298. *Id.*
299. FTC Press Release, *FTC Shuts Down Promoters of Deceptive Cryptocurrency Schemes*, ftc.gov, (Mar. 16, 2018).

FTC argued that few would benefit, and in fact, the majority would fail to recoup their initial investments.

According to the FTC, "participants could only generate revenue by recruiting new participants and convincing them to also pay cryptocurrency."[300] The FTC charged the defendants with violating the FTC Act's prohibition against deceptive acts from its misrepresentations of referrals as "bona fide money-making opportunities" and by "falsely claiming that participants could earn substantial income by participating in the three schemes."[301]

At the end of 2020, the FTC sued operators of a mobile-banking app for misleading users about access to their funds—which was supposed to be "24/7 access"—and for falsely promising them high interest rates.[302] Instead, the users had to wait weeks and sometimes months to receive their money. Other users never received their money.

Because of the defendant's failure to give the users their funds, the FTC asserted that they suffered "real financial harm, particularly for those who have lost income due to the COVID-19 pandemic," and the defendant thus violated the FTC Act's prohibitions against misrepresentations. In mid-May 2021, the FTC released a press release in which it unveiled data showing a "huge spike in cryptocurrency investment scams." Examples of such scams included fake celebrity endorsements and promises enticing customers to transfer cryptocurrencies or Elon Musk impersonators.[303]

The FTC has been active in prosecuting cryptocurrency-related scams and has had little trouble doing so under the existing regulations and consumer-protection statutes. The broad reach of the Federal Trade Commission Act has given the FTC wide latitude to bring enforcement actions against individuals or entities that use unfair or deceptive acts related to cryptocurrencies to harm consumers within the United States. It remains to be seen whether the FTC, or Congress, will introduce new laws or regulations that address cryptocurrencies, digital assets, or blockchain technology. But the future may bring a steady increase in the number and sophistication of the FTC's enforcement actions against these types of scams.

300. *Id.*
301. *Id.*
302. FTC Press Release, *FTC Alleges Mobile Banking App Misled Users About Access to Their Funds, Failed to Deliver on Promised High Interest Rates* ftc.gov, (Nov. 18, 2020).
303. FTC Press Release, *FTC Data Shows Huge Spike in Cryptocurrency Investment Scams,* ftc.gov, (May 17, 2021).

5. BLOCKCHAIN, CRYPTOCURRENCY, AND AML

The United States expects companies to implement robust compliance programs and AML policies to prevent financial violations. The U.S. tax system also depends on the voluntary reporting of taxpayers. This applies with equal force to cryptocurrency transactions. Legislation in the United States has had a rocky history in encouraging voluntary reporting vs. criminal prosecutions. But beginning in 2009, the United States implemented the Offshore Voluntary Disclosure Program (OVDP),[304] by which taxpayers with undisclosed foreign accounts could avoid criminal prosecutions by coming forward, disclosing their foreign accounts, and paying lesser penalties. OVAP yielded successful results.

In 2010, Congress passed the Foreign Account Tax Compliance Act (FATCA),[305] which is another tool used by the IRS to avoid tax avoidance in foreign jurisdictions. FATCA requires foreign institutions to identify and disclose information about U.S. account holders to the IRS. Since foreign exchanges and virtual-wallet providers are unregulated to begin with, FATCA may not work well with crypto disclosures. As a result, many are calling for a program like OVAP for voluntary crypto disclosures.[306]

Federal legislation intended to prevent money laundering and fraud also applies to blockchain-based platforms. For instance, the Bank Secrecy Act (BSA)[307] and the PATRIOT Act impose various requirements on financial institutions.[308] AML/KYC policies protect financial institutions from being used to facilitate financial crime. Failure to comply with these policies can lead to serious penalties, including asset seizures, criminal asset forfeiture, jail time, or fines. Criminal asset forfeiture under 21 U.S. Code § 853 provides the following:

---

304. *United States and Switzerland Agree on Access to Swiss Bank Information,* 103 AMERICAN JOURNAL OF INTERNATIONAL LAW 4, 748-750, (Feb. 27, 2017).
305. IRS, Foreign Account Tax Compliance Act (FATCA) irs.gov, (last visited April 22, 2022), available at https://www.irs.gov/businesses/corporations/foreign-account-tax-compliance-act-fatca
306. CASEY W. BAKER, RALPH E. MCKINNEY, JR., *Cryptocurrency and Federal Tax Enforcement,* American Bar Association, Business Law Today, 2021.
307. 31 U.S.C. § 5311 et seq. See also, Office of the Comptroller of the Currency, Bank Secrecy Act (BSA), (last visited April 22, 2022), available at https://www.occ.treas.gov/topics/supervision-and-examination/bsa/index-bsa.html
308. H.R.3162 – *Uniting and Strengthening America by Providing Appropriate Tools Required to Intercept and Obstruct Terrorism (USA PATRIOT ACT) Act of 200,1* (last visited April 22, 2022), available at https://www.congress.gov/107/plaws/publ56/PLAW-107publ56.pdf

> Any person convicted of a violation [of this section] punishable by imprisonment for more than one year shall forfeit to the United States, irrespective of any provision of State law (1) any property constituting, or derived from, any proceeds the person obtained, directly or indirectly, as the result of such violation, (2) any of the person's property used, or intended to be used, in any manner or part, to commit, or to facilitate the commission of, such violation, and (3) in the case of a person convicted of engaging in a continuing criminal enterprise . . . , the person shall forfeit, in addition to any property described in paragraph (1) or (2), any of his interest in, claims against, and property or contractual rights affording a source of control over, the continuing criminal enterprise.[309]

Former DOJ Trial Attorney John Sellers has stated that "cryptocurrency exchanges do not necessarily have to be "financial institutions" under Title 31 to be subject to the Bank Secrecy Act. Cryptocurrency exchanges come in all sorts of sizes and shapes and may be considered "money transmitters" or even "futures commission merchants" and fall within its scope."

The IRS and other federal agencies now have their eyes on offshore crypto exchanges. Some of these exchanges facilitate daily trades worth tens of billions of dollars. For instance, in 2020, federal prosecutors charged BitMEX, a foreign exchange for trading cryptocurrency derivatives, with criminal AML violations. The CFTC filed a parallel civil lawsuit alleging that BitMEX had received over $11 million in Bitcoin deposits from accounts with U.S. connections and has earned over $1 billion in fees since 2014.[310] BitMEX had failed to implement a customer information program, KYC procedures, and a sufficient AML program.[311] BitMEX was not the first instance of federal agency enforcement of crypto exchanges. In 2015, FinCEN alleged that Ripple Labs—the blockchain company that is also facing a lawsuit by the SEC for an unregistered securities offering—violated AML requirements and ordered Ripple to pay a $700,000 fine.[312] For now, it is uncertain whether existing legislation will be enough to prevent crypto money laundering. But the IRS and other federal agencies are aware of these activities, and it may be just a matter of time before Congress brings blockchain-based

309. 21 U.S.C. Code § 853.
310. DAVE MICHAELS, *BitMEX Co-Founders Charged with U.S. Rules Violations,* THE WALL STREET JOURNAL, wsj.com, (Oct. 1, 2020).
311. CFTC Release 8412-21, *Federal Court Orders BitMEX to Pay $100 Million for Illegally Operating a Cryptocurrency Trading Platform and Anti-Money Laundering Violations,* cftc.gov, (Aug. 10, 2021).
312. FINCEN, *FinCEN Fines Ripple Labs Inc. in First Civil Enforcement Action Against a Virtual Currency Exchanger,* fincen.gov, (May 5, 2015).

businesses and decentralized exchanges explicitly within the scope of federal anti-money-laundering provisions.

SUMMARY

The federal government's authority over blockchain technology and cryptocurrencies is expanding. The SEC is determining whether some coins or tokens may be securities that fall within its jurisdiction. Once a securities link is found, no matter how small, the SEC can regulate all market participants involved with that asset. For instance, the SEC can regulate a broker that sells the security asset and anything else for their clients, a company that invests in the security asset for its shareholders, and exchanges that trade the security asset after initial issuance.[313]

The IRS is using John Doe summonses and the fear of prosecution against private companies to compel tax compliance. The CFTC is also trying to regulate digital-asset derivatives and digital-asset commodities, and FinCEN aims to ensure that money transmitters are following AML laws for digital assets. Private lawsuits may also be on the rise, but it is government investigations that will lead the way in regulating digital assets to benefit investors, the market, and the United States. It remains to be seen how far the government is willing to go to achieve this goal.

313. TODD PHILLIPS, *The SEC's Regulatory Role in the Digital Asset Markets,* americanprogress.org, (Oct. 4, 2021).

PART 3:

BLOCKCHAIN AND THE FUTURE PRACTICE OF LAW

"Digital assets are here to stay in our financial system, and the decisions we make now will have impacts far into the future . . . We need to be fostering innovation, not stifling it, if we are going to maintain America's position as the global financial leader."

U.S. Senator Cynthia Lummis, Wyoming[314]

314. CYNTHIA LUMMIS, Senator for Wyoming, *Wyden & Lummis introduce Bill to Fix Broker Definition for Digital Assets*, lummis.senate.gov, (Nov. 15, 2021).

§ 12 Innovation in the Legal Profession

The introduction of technological innovations has disrupted many professions, including the practice of law. But compared to other industries—such as advertising or real estate—the legal profession is not known for its eagerness to embrace change and innovation.

It was only in 2012 that the American Bar Association amended Rule 1.1 of its Model Rules of Professional Conduct to state that to maintain competence, "a lawyer should keep abreast of changes in the law and its practice, including the benefits and risks associated with relevant technology."[315]

1. TECHNOLOGY AND LAW

Law firms tend to be institutionally conservative. This is unsurprising given that the law itself changes slowly, and when change does occur, it usually happens incrementally via extensions of existing precedent. Radical, overnight changes are rare. For centuries, law school curricula have focused on teaching case law and legal theory—not so much marketplace analysis, business operations, and statistics.

As businesses, law firms tend to be more hesitant to go for new things without clear and convincing evidence that such an investment will improve their revenue. This risk aversion means that the typical driver of innovation, competition between firms, is muted in the legal profession. If tech start-ups are at one end of the spectrum, characterized by a risk-taking, failure-accepting attitude, law firms are closer to the opposite end. Former Assistant U.S. Attorney Lynette Byrd notes:

"We, as lawyers, tend to be more conservative, risk averse, and resistant to change. But as with the age of electronic-discovery, technology and law when merged can bring a level of ease and simplicity to projects, which might otherwise be daunting or even impossible. Especially

315. Model Rules of Prof'l Conduct R. 1.1 cmt. 8, (2012).

in large-scale investigations involving voluminous documents and information, blockchain technology should be a welcomed and encouraged participant in the legal arena."

Demographics also play a role. The senior partners who control a law firm's direction and business operations may defend the status quo, especially if they are nearing retirement. Why spend time and money fixing something that has worked for them in the past?

Regulatory restrictions can also hinder innovation in the market for legal services. Consider the examples of LegalZoom, Rocket Lawyer, and other online legal technology companies. These companies seek to provide low-cost legal services to individual consumers and small businesses that cannot afford to hire an attorney. Although these companies claim regulatory compliance, their nationwide online presence comes with challenges.

In 2007, the State Bar of North Carolina issued a cease-and-desist letter to LegalZoom, asserting that its activities in the state constituted the unauthorized practice of law. That dispute was resolved in 2015, when North Carolina's legislature passed a law that redefined the practice of law not to include the operation of a website like LegalZoom, which offers consumers access to interactive software that could generate legal documents based on the consumer's answers to certain questions.[316]

Yet even in jurisdictions where online operators are legally permitted to offer legal services, regulatory barriers limit the services they can provide. Proponents of these limitations usually argue that they are necessary to protect consumers. Others contend that the barriers' primary purpose is to protect lawyers' monopoly in the market for these services. Still, the effect is suppression of innovation—and deterrence.

Despite these obstacles, technological innovations have forced even the most stubborn luddites to adopt new technologies. Few lawyers today choose a typewriter over a computer or prefer the local law library over conducting an electronic search. Law and technology appear to be antithetical forces, yet they are two separate but conjoined halves of running a law practice.

2. A BRIEF HISTORY OF HOW TECHNOLOGY HAS DISRUPTED THE LEGAL PROFESSION

Next to typewriters, modern technology perhaps first disrupted the legal industry in the early 1950s when manufacturers began marketing

316. N.C. GEN. STAT. § 84-2.2 (2016).

dictation machines to law firms.[317] The early dictation machines were expensive, bulky, and prone to breaking down.

Before the 1970s, lawyers researched legal questions by reading physical treatises, hornbooks, and case reports. But in 1973, Lexis invented the "UBIQ" terminal, which allowed lawyers to research case law electronically.[318] Dedicated word-processing computers entered the scene to streamline their business. Although lawyers typically delegated word processing to secretaries, the result was more efficiency. By the late 1980s, fax machines became omnipresent.

In 1982, IBM released the Personal Computer (PC). Lawyers began to learn word processing so they could create documents and spreadsheets. Along with the PC came computer applications such as contact-managing software, calendars, and document databases. Case-management systems emerged. Some early competitors were minicomputers and Apple Computer, Inc.'s Macintosh. But these machines were expensive and not always user-friendly.

A decade later, Microsoft released Windows 3.1, which supplanted the older DOS machines. True to form, law firms were not at the forefront in migrating to Windows. While developers were providing Windows applications, legal vendors continued to focus on DOS upgrades. But by the mid to late 1990s, most law firms had transitioned to Windows. By 1995, a range of Windows legal applications were available, such as software for case management, time and billing, and docketing, as well as various specialized tools for specific practices such as intellectual property and real estate.[319]

Internet and online services marked the point of no return. Computers have become essential. Websites, emails, online marketing, e-discovery, and social media are all part of a contemporary lawyer's reservoir of tools.

But no technology is without challenges. Computer viruses, hacking, spam, spyware, and issues of online reputation management are some of the negative side effects that have accompanied the technological boom. Yet information technology has irreversibly changed the way law firms do business.

317. SMOKEBALL, *A (Very) Brief History of Legal Technology,* smokeball.com, (Jan. 30, 2020).

318. RON FRIEDMANN, *Back to the Future: A History of Legal Technology,* AmLaw Tech, (Dec. 2004), available at https://prismlegal.com/back_to_the_future-a-history-of-legal-technology/

319. *Id.*

§ 13 How Blockchain Impacts the Legal Profession

Blockchain is the next technology that lawyers shouldn't ignore. Mainstream acceptance of blockchain is pending, and the opportunities to expand a lawyer's practice are rich. This section summarizes Part 2 and reiterates some feasible blockchain innovations in transactional law, litigation, corporate advice, regulatory compliance, and white-collar defense. While some ideas may be too futuristic, other ideas are already ripe for implementation.

1. SMART CONTRACTS

At its most basic, a smart contract is a self-executing computer program contained within a decentralized blockchain network. The key features of smart contracts are transparency, immutability, and efficiency.

With more industries integrating smart contracts into their operations, lawyers should educate themselves on the workings and risks of these new applications. Two schools of thought exist.

Some suggest that smart contracts could replace traditional contracts and with it, lawyers. Although the code of a smart contract could hypothetically contain the terms of a legally binding contract, most instances of smart contracts still require a traditional contract that incorporates the smart contract.

Thus, it is more likely that smart contracts will operate in tandem with written contracts. For example, ICOs often use a smart contract to facilitate the collection of virtual currency and the distribution of the new digital token. This process is complemented by a written agreement that sets out the risks assumed by the purchasers and any rights they may have against the vendor. Modern transactional lawyers must understand how to combine traditional and smart contracts in a legally binding document.

In the context of transactional law, clients will also need advice on regulatory compliance and enforceability. Smart contracts may become a factor in existing industries, such as data storage and e-commerce that operates within existing regulatory frameworks. For clients' business proposals to work, they must be structured correctly. Projects that rely on smart contracts will require lawyers' help to ensure the business proposal stays within the confines of existing or evolving regulations.

Lawyers may find smart contracts useful for their own organizations. For example, a firm may hold funds in escrow in connection with a client's business transaction or as part of a settlement negotiation. By using a smart contract, a firm may automate, or even eliminate, the escrow process by deploying a program that transfers funds to the appropriate parties once the obligations under the agreement are performed. If one side fails to perform, the smart contract could return funds to the other party.

Similarly, smart contracts may facilitate client invoicing by transferring funds from a linked client trust account to the firm's operating account. While other firms spend valuable time and resources processing invoices and chasing down clients, a firm that integrates smart contracts into this process can reduce fee disputes. Additionally, most law firms need to track and maintain a variety of data, such as client information, case files, and transaction histories. Smart contracts and blockchain technology allow firms to record data securely. A firm could use a data-management system integrated with smart contracts to keep these records in an immutable, transparent, and secure manner. This would strengthen the protection of sensitive client information.

2. INTELLECTUAL PROPERTY

Blockchain technology is a natural fit for intellectual-property connoisseurs. Because blockchains create unalterable data, intellectual-property owners can establish the authenticity of ownership rights, combat counterfeiting, license property through smart contracts, and efficiently register trademarks by using blockchain technology.

Intellectual-property holders often find it difficult to establish ownership of a copyrighted work or show that another party has infringed their work. Similarly, third parties may struggle to know from whom to seek a license.

Blockchain technology can serve as an intellectual-property registry that catalogs and stores original works. This registry could provide creators with secure digital certificates that verify the nature of a work and the origination time. These digital certificates could establish that a particular work was created by the artist at a specific time and simultaneously allow for authentication and validation of an intellectual-property asset, exposing any infringement on the copyright.

A ledger that shows the ownership of a given piece of intellectual property can distinguish counterfeit or unlicensed works from the original, which is even more significant because of the widespread digitization of copyrighted material. By registering newly created intellectual property, such as a piece of music, a work of art, or a design on a blockchain-based registry, an owner can establish unimpeachable ownership of the work's copyright.

Replacing traditional centralized registration systems with decentralized systems will make it easier to register new intellectual property, update filings, and transfer ownership in a secure manner at any time. Future inventors may integrate their intellectual property into a blockchain for patenting purposes. If a dispute arises, the patenting authority can track the ownership of the patented object by examining the blockchain.

Blockchain and smart contracts can be used in tandem to efficiently license intellectual property, allowing authors and licensees to interface directly without needing an intermediary. Additionally, the smart contract could be self-executing upon the use of the work, thereby ensuring prompt payment to the author for any use of the licensed asset.

One example of this application is the blockchain-based platform Mycelia, which provides a decentralized musical database for artists to share music and receive payment for the use of their works. Another example, although ultimately unsuccessful, was Kodak's attempt to launch a blockchain-based image rights-management platform for photographers called KODAKOne in 2018.[320] The platform sought to provide an encrypted, digital ledger of rights ownership for photographers to register works and license them within the platform. The platform also intended to provide continual web crawling to monitor and protect images that were registered on the system. While KODAKOne may have failed, it is likely just a matter of time until someone makes a more successful attempt at a blockchain-based image-rights platform.

The integration of blockchain and intellectual property may be closer to reality than you think. Governments around the world are engaging in pilot projects to test how blockchain technologies might assist their intellectual-property functions.

---

320. Kodak Press Release, *KODAK and WENN Digital Partner to Launch Major Blockchain Initiative and Cryptocurrency,* kodak.com, (Jan. 9, 2018).

In March 2020, the U.S. Customs and Border Protection (CBP) announced that it had completed a proof-of-concept of a blockchain platform to protect American businesses from intellectual-property theft.[321] The platform could enable communication between manufacturers, retailers, rights holders, and importers to help prevent the importation of counterfeit products into the United States. According to the CBP, the platform allowed it to identify and link a product to its license, requiring fewer physical examinations.

Previously, the European Union Intellectual Property Office announced the launch of Europe's first-ever blockchain platform for the secure delivery of intellectual-property-rights documentation in real time.[322] This platform will allow creators to register their intellectual property onto a blockchain and combat counterfeiting. Again, blockchain technology may be so integrated into intellectual property that IP lawyers will need, at minimum, a basic understanding of its functions to properly advise clients.

3. CORPORATE FILINGS

Corporate filings and other records may soon be maintained on blockchain platforms. In a sense, a corporation is just its records. It is possible to have every corporate document and transaction recorded on a blockchain so that there is an immutable record of all corporate acts.

In 2017, Delaware amended its law to allow companies to maintain their corporate records using blockchain technology. Given that Delaware is one of the nation's prime corporate situs, this amendment is a significant step toward widespread use of blockchain for corporate records.

Governments may eventually provide blockchain platforms for companies to submit their corporate registrations and documents. This will create a permanent, immutable, and transparent record of any changes. Corporate lawyers may need to learn about blockchain technology to advise their clients on the logistics, benefits, and risks of corporate record keeping through blockchain.

4. CRIMINAL CASES

The criminal justice system stands to benefit from blockchain. Criminal cases involve voluminous documents and records, all of which must be authenticated, recorded, and stored securely. Sometimes, it is also

321. LEDGER INSIGHTS, *U.S. Customs Tests Blockchain for Intellectual Property Protection,* ledgerinsights.com, (March 3, 2020).
322. EUIPO, *EUIPO Connects to TMview and DesignView Through Blockchain*, euipo.europa.eu, (April 27, 2021).

vital that the chain of custody for documents or items can be accurately tracked. Hypothetically, from the moment a defendant is cited or arrested, case information could be recorded onto a blockchain. Former Justice Department lawyer Lynette Byrd explains:

> Historically, the legal profession is constantly playing "catch up" to technology. Even more so, the government - particularly through its regulatory and enforcement framework - is always trying to catch up with innovations of business and even more so, of criminal enterprise. For example, as part of criminal investigations, federal agencies monitored phone and email traffic through normative platforms for years. So instead, people turned to using alternatives like WhatsApp or Signal. Similarly, entrepreneurs and others ventured into the unknown realm of the crypto space before the government was ready for it. But the government is catching on quickly; we have already begun to see examples of cases in which federal agents in connection with DOJ are seizing digital wallets and other non-traditional currency in criminal cases.

As the case proceeds through the judicial system, each participant updates the single blockchain record with their actions, for example, the initial arrest record, indictment, and plea. These blockchain-based records can be shared with defense counsel, government attorneys, law-enforcement officers, parole officers, the court, and even victims or witnesses when appropriate. Changes show instantly and to all relevant parties.

Logging cases and their records onto a blockchain would enhance public access to information while ensuring secure and reliable record keeping. The reliability of blockchain-based records may become the standard for determining whether critical evidence is admissible at trial. Both criminal defense attorneys and prosecutors may need to be familiar with the technology, its capabilities, and its limitations to do their jobs effectively.

5. PROOF OF SERVICE

Lawyers have traditionally relied on process servers to deliver court documents. While most process servers are honest and trustworthy individuals, a few are not. In 2008, for example, a scandal shook the process-serving industry in New York.[323]

New York City's Department of Consumer Affairs found that certain process-serving companies were filing false affidavits of service. The

---

323. ROBERT AMBROGI, *Wondering How Blockchain Can Be Used in Legal? Here's One: Service of Process,* lawsitesblog.com, (Feb. 9, 2018).

so-called "sewer service" scandal led to stricter rules for service of process in New York.

Blockchain may make service abuse impossible. Hypothetically, blockchain technology could provide courts, lawyers, and parties access to verifiable, tamper-proof information about service of process. When the server makes or attempts service, the server uploads mobile data including GPS coordinates, a timestamp, and certain other metadata, such as the device used. That record, which may include images of the papers served and how they were delivered, would be given a unique blockchain ID that can subsequently be viewed by anyone with access to the blockchain platform. Ultimately, it is conceivable for blockchain technology to eliminate human proof and manual delivery of service.

6. LITIGATION AND SETTLEMENT

Civil litigation is notorious for the number of documents exchanged and records created. It includes the various activities before, during, and after a lawsuit is filed, such as investigation, negotiation, trial, and post-judgment procedures.

Why not record the entire litigation process, including discovery, on a blockchain platform? It could become standard practice for lawyers to register themselves onto a blockchain platform with their personal information, license number, and details about their experience or area of practice.

The platform may allow a client to search for and select an attorney. Lawyers may file complaints directly onto the blockchain, from which defense counsel could then access the complaint. Every subsequent document, from court orders to a jury verdict, could be recorded onto the same blockchain.

Such a platform would have to be established by the courts or other governmental bodies, like the PACER and the CM/ECF systems. Expect the first versions of these blockchain-based platforms to emerge in private dispute resolution settings, likely international arbitration.

7. BLOCKCHAIN-BASED ARBITRATION

In the twentieth century, arbitration became a popular method for businesses to resolve disputes without engaging in litigation. Arbitration promised to be a faster, easier process that would permit the parties to select expert adjudicators in their field rather than trusting the luck of the draw for a general civil judge or jury to resolve their dispute. The combination of blockchain and arbitration might offer several advantages.

A blockchain system provides an organized record of all filed items. Many aspects of the arbitration process, such as documentary evidence, transmittal of correspondence, and satisfaction of awards, could be automated with smart contracts. Even the appointment of the arbitrator could be done through blockchain when the parties agree on a process and a smart contract executes the selection. Blockchain-based arbitration could also offer enhanced confidentiality. Even in an arbitration proceeding intended to be confidential, there is always a risk that documents may be leaked or stolen by hackers. Blockchain can alleviate such concerns.

Blockchain-based arbitration could also pave the way for automated dispute resolution, especially in the context of smart contracts. An arbitral method and decision could be agreed upon by the parties and deployed directly onto the blockchain, permitting a self-executing and automatic arbitral award. Or the disputed smart contract could have an arbitral algorithm integrated directly into the agreement so that it can resolve the dispute itself, within the parameters of the agreement. Admittedly, many questions remain before blockchain-based arbitration becomes commonplace, not the least of which is whether such an arbitral award is even enforceable.

8. E-DISCOVERY

Whether in the form of smart contracts, blockchain-based record keeping, supply-chain management, or licensing, the mere fact that clients are using this technology means that, once a dispute arises, blockchain-based information will become discoverable as electronically stored information.

Lawyers must be prepared for this possibility by developing their understanding of blockchain-based data storage and designing protocols for handling this data. In general, data stored on a blockchain has several attractive features for litigators, including permanence and a record of changes over time. Yet the fact that blockchain transactions are pseudonymous can make it difficult to prove the identity of participants in a transaction. Lawyers may need to spend time and resources consulting the proper custodians to establish identities and decode blockchain transactions. Additionally, while there are tools to track blockchain activities, they may not translate well to evidence that is viewable on most e-discovery software platforms.

Although data stored on a blockchain is reliable, it must be transferred from the blockchain to make it accessible and usable as evidence. Parties will therefore need to authenticate how they are providing blockchain-based data in discovery. To avoid unnecessary expenses later, lawyers should discuss information-governance considerations with their corporate clients early on to help them develop policies for their blockchain-based data systems that facilitate disclosure in the event of discoverability in a later dispute. Lawyers should also stay updated on how courts handle future blockchain e-discovery issues, as these decisions will provide critical guidance on clients' duties in terms of their blockchain data.

9. PROPERTY RIGHTS

Just like IP rights, physical-property rights could also be stored digitally on a blockchain platform.

In the United States, land ownership is recorded at the local level, usually by a county recorder's office or a tax assessor's office. This process often relies on paper documentation vulnerable to loss, fraud, or mismanagement. Because the process for registering ownership of property differs between states and involves small localities, it is unlikely that a unified, digital, nationwide land registry will be adopted any time soon.

Yet some forward-thinking states or counties may perceive the advantages of such a land registry and begin implementing this technology in the coming years. Blockchain is well suited to track the sale of real estate because its data-storage records transfers and transactions over time, simplifying ownership searches and title checks.

By using a distributed ledger, governments can also more easily publish data transparently, which will help parties track property-related legal matters such as encumbrances, liens, and easements. Ultimately, blockchain-based land registries could facilitate market transactions and promote economic growth. The adoption of blockchain-based land registries may alter the way real-estate attorneys assist clients.

10. FINANCIAL TRANSACTIONS

Blockchain adds transparency in the financial-services industry. By performing transactions on a public ledger, inefficiencies and fraud are easier to detect and address.

One primary concern with digital transactions is the risk of hacking or scams. Blockchain technology can increase the security of transactions. Transfers made on the blockchain are faster and more traceable than traditional banking transactions. The elimination of intermediaries can also lower costs, making it easier to transfer funds around the world. New platforms that facilitate transactions via blockchain technology are already emerging and present a credible alternative to existing financial services.

The DeFi industry, for example, seeks to supplant existing financial services by providing decentralized exchanges and lending platforms. That said, it appears more likely that existing financial institutions will integrate and capitalize on blockchain technology rather than allow start-up DeFi platforms to replace them entirely. Still, the implementation of blockchain technology into the financial services industries will present new legal challenges for lawyers to navigate.

11. ACCEPTING LEGAL FEES IN CRYPTOCURRENCY

Some law firms are already accepting payment in cryptocurrency. If you haven't already, you may soon encounter clients who wish to pay you in cryptocurrency instead of traditional currency. Although cryptocurrency is not the only application of blockchain technology, it has achieved a lot of notoriety. As of January 10, 2022, the total value of all cryptocurrencies was about $1.9 trillion, a decline from $2.9 trillion at its peak in 2021.[324]

Before accepting cryptocurrency as payment, you must understand the legal implications of such transfers. Although cryptocurrencies can store value, they do not usually meet the definition of money. Cryptocurrencies are more like valuable forms of property like gold, art, stock certificates, and other assets. As a result, you should think of cryptocurrency as stored valuable assets rather than money.

Because cryptocurrency is not money, it cannot be stored at an ordinary bank. To process cryptocurrency transactions within your law firm, you will need to obtain a wallet for the cryptocurrencies that you plan to accept, such as Bitcoin or Ethereum. There are two primary types of cryptocurrency wallets: hardware wallets and web wallets.[325]

A hardware wallet collects your transaction information from the internet and stores it on a local device. When such a wallet is disconnected from the network, it is usually known as a "cold" wallet. The benefit of a cold wallet is that because it is disconnected, it cannot be accessed by unauthorized users. A cold wallet becomes "hot" when it is connected to the network to process a transaction, after which it can again be safely disconnected.

The benefit of keeping a wallet hot is that it is usually more accessible and easier to use in internet transactions. To buy something or receive payment in cryptocurrency, using a hot wallet makes the process

324. KEVIN VOIGT & ANDY ROSEN, *Cryptocurrency: What It Is and How It Works,* nerdwallet.com, (Jun. 13, 2022).

325. TERESA MATICH, *How to Accept Bitcoin at Your Law Firm,* clio.com, (Nov. 10, 2021).

simpler. Yet because the wallet is hot, both the private and public keys for the wallet are stored online or on a device that is connected to the internet. This means that the keys might be vulnerable to hackers, so you should take special precautions to ensure your information cannot be stolen. As a security measure, you may consider maintaining both hot and cold wallets. The bulk of your assets should be stored on the cold wallet, and only the portion needed to process transactions should be kept in the hot wallet.

As an alternative to a hardware wallet, you may wish to use a web wallet, also known as an online wallet. Web wallets are cloud-based wallets often hosted by a third-party platform like a cryptocurrency exchange. Web wallets are always hot, with the advantages and disadvantages mentioned above. The main advantage of web wallets is that they can be accessed anywhere and from any device. They also tend to be very user-friendly and can rapidly transfer funds between different types of cryptocurrency or different exchanges. Web wallets have even more security vulnerabilities than standard hot wallets. For example, web wallets may fall victim to malware, phishing scams, DDoS attacks, and other forms of hacking. Some popular web wallet providers include Coinbase, Gemini, Robinhood, Blockchain, and Crypto.com.

Whether you use a web wallet, a hardware wallet, or some combination of the two, most clients will transfer cryptocurrency to you quickly. The most important thing for your firm is to choose a wallet that complies with any applicable state or federal regulations. That is why it is important to do your due diligence and select a reputable wallet with a solid compliance record.

Ethical requirements can also thwart accepting cryptocurrency for fees. Lawyers cannot charge unreasonable fees. Since the value of a cryptocurrency can change over short periods, holding a client's cryptocurrency could result in an unreasonably large fee. The simplest way to avoid this possibility is to convert any cryptocurrencies you receive into fiat. After receiving a transfer of cryptocurrency into your wallet, you will need to use a payment processer, such as a cryptocurrency exchange, to convert your assets into traditional currency. At this stage, it is important to again do your due diligence and ensure that the service you use complies with any applicable regulations. Only after you have converted the cryptocurrency into money can you deposit the funds into your business account.

Money laundering is another concern. Be careful with unknown or suspicious sources of funds—even more so in the context of cryptocurrency payments. Apply extra caution with funds from third parties. Follow procedures from your engagement letter along these lines:

> The Client represents that all funds payable or paid to the Firm originate from lawful income or lawful U.S. sources and are not subject to garnishment, forfeiture, seizure, money laundering, or bankruptcy proceedings. Client represents that Client is not aware at the time of any transfer that any government agency has asserted that the specific funds transferred to Firm are subject to, among others, forfeiture. By and through Client's signature below, Client acknowledges that Client has discussed this provision with Firm, that Firm has an obligation to conduct reasonable due diligence under Section 9-120.100 et seq. of the U.S. Attorney's Manual to determine whether there are any reasonable grounds that would prohibit the receipt of legal funds from Client at the time of transfer, and that Client has sufficient uncontested resources with which to pay Firm's fees and expenses in the Matter.

Finally, you may be asked to hold cryptocurrency in trust for your clients. Unfortunately, unlike traditional money, you cannot transfer digital currency into your traditional trust account. In this circumstance, you should avoid converting the cryptocurrency into fiat currency because there is a chance one might be helping launder illegal proceeds or diminishing your client's fees through conversion.

Instead, notify your client that you will not be converting their assets and explain that it may lose value while you are holding it in trust. Your client must understand that the value of the cryptocurrency may change while it is in your possession and that you are not responsible for any loss in value, which may be grounds for discipline or even disbarment.

You must also take appropriate security measures to protect your client's cryptocurrency. This might include using a cold wallet to store assets, using multi-signature accounts, or further encrypting the private key used to transfer the cryptocurrency. Additionally, you should review your local bar rules and any applicable state or federal regulations to ensure that your cryptocurrency-storage procedures follow relevant law.

12. GOVERNMENT ENFORCEMENT

Governments around the world are taking notice of the increase in blockchain-based ventures, particularly in cryptocurrency. In October 2021, for example, the DOJ announced that it would enhance its scrutiny of the cryptocurrency market by creating a National Cryptocurrency Enforcement Team (NCET).[326]

---

326. DOJ Press Release 21-974, *Deputy Attorney General Lisa O. Monaco Announces National Cryptocurrency Enforcement Team*, justice.gov, (Oct. 6, 2021).

The NCET intends to pursue criminal investigations and actions against cryptocurrency misuse by focusing on crimes committed by virtual currency exchanges, mixing and tumbling services, and money-laundering infrastructure actors. The team also plans to assist in the tracing and recovery of assets lost because of fraud and extortion, including cryptocurrency payments to ransomware groups. According to the DOJ, NCET "will also play a critical support role for international, federal, state, local, tribal, and territorial law-enforcement authorities grappling with these new technologies and new forms of criminal tradecraft."[327]

NCET will coordinate the sharing of information between law-enforcement offices to maximize the effectiveness of DOJ investigations, prosecutions, and forfeitures involving cryptocurrency. The creation of NCET comes in the wake of several DOJ enforcement actions that concerned cryptocurrency. These actions include embezzlement, ransomware attacks, securities fraud, money laundering, theft, and violations of international law. Both prosecutors and defense attorneys should expect to encounter cases that concern cryptocurrency assets, which is why it is essential to be familiar with this technology. These examples of recent DOJ enforcement actions establish that cryptocurrency-related cases are a current and growing portion of the legal landscape.

a. Darknet Funding

In October 2019, a federal grand jury in the District of Columbia indicted a South Korean national, Jong Woo Son, for operating the largest-ever child sexual-exploitation market by volume of content.[328] According to the indictment, Son operated a Darknet market that advertised child sexual-exploitation videos and made them available for download. Members of the site could purchase videos by using Bitcoin, and each user received a unique Bitcoin address when the user created an account on the site. IRS special agents traced these Bitcoin transactions, enabling them to determine the location of the server hosting the website, identify the website's administrator, and track down the server's physical location in South Korea. This case reveals that tracking cryptocurrency transactions is central to modern law enforcement.

327. *Id.*

328. DOJ Press Release 19-1,104, *South Korean National and Hundreds of Others Charged Worldwide in the Takedown of the Largest Darknet Child Pornography Website, Which was Funded by Bitcoin,* justice.gov, (Oct. 16, 2019)

b. Evading International Sanctions

United States law prohibits the exportation of any goods, services, or technology to North Korea without a license from the Treasury Department. In December 2019, the DOJ charged U.S. citizen Virgil Griffith with violating this law by traveling to North Korea to deliver a presentation and technical advice on using cryptocurrency and blockchain technology to evade sanctions.[329] According to the DOJ, Griffith traveled to North Korea for this exact purpose, despite receiving warnings not to go. The complaint alleged that Griffith attended and presented at the "Pyongyang Blockchain and Cryptocurrency Conference," knowing that by doing so he was violating U.S. sanctions against North Korea. Although such cases may be rare, Griffith's prosecution shows how cryptocurrency and blockchain technology can be used to aid and abet not only individual international criminals but also state adversaries like North Korea, Iran, and Russia.

c. Hacking

In July 2020, about 130 high-profile Twitter accounts were compromised after hackers gained access to Twitter's administrative tools. This allowed them to tweet directly from the compromised accounts. The compromised accounts included those of well-known individuals such as Elon Musk, Barack Obama, Bill Gates, Jeff Bezos, Michael Bloomberg, Warren Buffet, Kanye West, and companies such as Apple, Wendy's, Uber, and Cash App.[330] The hackers tweeted out requests that people send Bitcoin to a specific cryptocurrency wallet and promised that any money sent would be doubled and returned. Within minutes, hundreds of transactions had taken place and more than $110,000 had been deposited into the receiving account. On July 31, 2020, the DOJ announced that it had arrested and charged three individuals responsible for the scam.[331] Cybercrime experts within the DOJ had analyzed the blockchain transactions and identified the hackers responsible for the scam.

---

329. DOJ Press Release 19-1322, *Department of Justice Announces Arrest of United States Citizen for Assisting North Korea in Evading Sanctions,* justice.gov, (Dec. 2, 2019).

330. DAVID INGRAM & KEVIN COLLIER, *Biden, Gates, Musk: Bitcoin Scam Breaches Some of World's Most Prominent Twitter Accounts,* nbcnews.com, (July 16, 2020).

331. DOJ Press Release 20-738, *Three Individuals Charged for Alleged Roles in Twitter Hack,* justice.gov, (July 31, 2020).

d. Seizure of Virtual Currency

The DOJ has also been active in seizing virtual currency that relates to criminal activity. In November 2020, for example, the DOJ announced that it had seized over $24 million worth of virtual currency on behalf of the government of Brazil.[332] According to documents and findings in the Brazilian criminal proceeding, Marcos Antonio Fagundes, a Brazilian citizen, fraudulently solicited funds from prospective investors over the internet. Fagundes and other conspirators allegedly operated their investment scheme without licenses and made false and inconsistent promises to investors about how they were using the funds. Upon request from the government of Brazil, the DOJ seized the virtual currency belonging to Fagundes that was in the United States. According to the DOJ press release, a cryptocurrency firm in the United States was holding the relevant accounts and cooperated with law-enforcement authorities to execute the seizure.

e. Securities Fraud

Securities-fraud cases about cryptocurrency have also been an active part of the DOJ's recent work. In February 2021, the DOJ charged John DeMarr, a California man, for allegedly participating in a coordinated cryptocurrency- and securities-fraud scheme.[333] The indictment alleges that DeMarr persuaded investors to pour millions of dollars into fraudulent cryptocurrency schemes only to divert the funds for his personal use. Investors sent millions of dollars' worth of Bitcoin, Ethereum, and fiat currency to financial accounts, including cryptocurrency wallets, controlled by DeMarr and others. According to the DOJ, DeMarr promised investors an 8,000% annual return on their investments. DeMarr then allegedly staged his own disappearance to avoid being confronted by disgruntled investors. Yet IRS criminal investigators in Los Angeles tracked him down. The case serves as a cautionary tale for the dangers of predatory investment schemes that permeate the cryptocurrency space. When advising clients, lawyers should encourage them to do their due diligence before transferring funds to any purported investment scheme. In most cases, if it sounds too good to be true, it is.

---

332. DOJ Press Release 20-1201, *U.S. Seizes Virtual Currencies Valued at $24 Million Assisting Brazil in Major Internet Fraud Investigation,* justice.gov, (Nov. 4, 2020).

333. DOJ Press Release 21-120, *U.S.-Based Promoter of Foreign Cryptocurrency Companies Charged in over $11 Million Securities Fraud Scheme,* justice.gov, (Feb. 1, 2021).

f. Ransomware

Ransomware, a type of malware, has gained significant popularity among criminal actors in recent years. In most cases, ransomware threatens either to publish a victim's personal data or to permanently block the victim's access to certain data unless a ransom is paid. Although it has gained popularity recently, the first ransomware scams date back to as early as 1989.[334] The DOJ has been actively targeting ransomware scammers, and their cases often involve cryptocurrency. For instance, in June 2021, the DOJ announced that it had seized 63.7 bitcoins, with a value of around $2.3 million, from a group known as Darkside.[335] Darkside had allegedly extorted the bitcoins from Colonial Pipeline, an American oil pipeline system, after gaining access to its computer network. By reviewing the transaction history on the public ledger, law enforcement tracked multiple transfers of Bitcoin and confirmed that the proceeds of the victim's ransom payment had been transferred to a specific address, which they were then able to seize.

g. Embezzlement

Because it is seen as secure and anonymous, cryptocurrency can become implicated in otherwise typical financial crimes. In 2021, for example, an employee of Sony Life Insurance Company in Tokyo, Rei Ishii, diverted about $154 million into a personal bank account in La Jolla, California. Ishii allegedly did this by falsifying transaction instructions, which caused the funds to be diverted. After the funds were transferred, Ishii converted the funds into Bitcoin to conceal the theft. In coordination with Sony, Citibank, and Japanese law enforcement, the FBI tracked down and recovered the bitcoins traceable to the theft. According to the DOJ's press release, the FBI recovered the funds because the victim acted quickly to contact law enforcement and because the FBI coordinated with Japanese law enforcement to identify the perpetrator. The rising popularity of cryptocurrency and its reputation for anonymity and security make it attractive to criminals as a potential way to hide stolen proceeds.

13. THE FUTURE OF THE LEGAL PROFESSION

Going forward, artificial intelligence, big data, predictive analytics, cloud computing, and other technologies will govern the way we do business.

---

334. KIERAN LAFFAN, *A Brief History of Ransomware,* varonis.com, (last updated Nov. 10, 2015).
335. DOJ Press Release 21-528, *Department of Justice Seizes $2.3 Million in Cryptocurrency Paid to the Ransomware Extortionists Darkside,* justice. Gov, (Jun. 7, 2021).

Blockchain technology is only one among many potential developments that could, within the next few years, upend the status quo for law firms. Firms should maintain a big-picture and long-term view of how these new tools can expand the scope of their practices. Firms should also be prepared for how their clients' adoption of these new technologies will affect not only the operation of the clients' businesses, but the type of advice and counsel that those clients will need. Given that blockchain technology has only been around for about a decade, there are still new applications of the technology that are yet to be discovered. Just how deeply this technology will impact the practice of law is difficult to say. What is clear, however, is that it is valuable, and perhaps necessary, for lawyers to learn about and understand these technologies. By staying on the cutting edge of these developments, law firms can obtain a competitive advantage over peers slower to adapt to the new environment. Whether firms are prepared for it or not, blockchain technology will be impacting every area of legal practice sooner than might be expected.

Intellectual property is on the brink of a transformation thanks to blockchain registries and smart contracts. Blockchain can streamline real-estate transactions and land registry. Litigators may find their practices affected in several ways, including changes to chain of custody, proof of service, e-discovery, and other litigation processes. Transactional attorneys are already called on to draft agreements that incorporate, or refer to, a corresponding smart contract. Corporate lawyers are advising their clients on how to structure their new blockchain companies to comply with various state and federal laws. Criminal attorneys are confronting several cases involving blockchain and cryptocurrencies, and tax lawyers are advising their clients on how to report the profits they've earned on cryptocurrency investments. Even family-law attorneys, who might not expect to have any connection to blockchain, are finding it relevant to their practices when they are asked to divide a husband and wife's cryptocurrency assets or when one party alleges that the other has diverted community assets into cryptocurrency assets held only in one party's name. The firms and individual attorneys that can best anticipate the ways these new technologies will change the legal profession will enjoy the greatest success.

CONCLUSION

This book provided a detailed overview of digital assets, beginning with a discussion of how the notions of trading evolved since ancient times and led to the creation of central banks, credit cards, stock markets, and digital currencies and tokens. One pivotal modern technological advance is the blockchain. The blockchain is a distributed public ledger where all cryptocurrency transactions are recorded and stored. These transactions are public and immutable, thus providing security and transparency. Bitcoin transactions, as well as other cryptocurrency transactions, are recorded on the blockchain.

Smart contracts were also discussed. Smart contracts represent a critical consequence of blockchain technology that allows virtually any application to be built onto a blockchain platform. While there are many advantages to smart contracts, they also have a few notable disadvantages. For instance, even though immutability can be an advantage in some cases, it is a disadvantage in others.

As blockchain technology and the use of crypto transactions grew in discussion and practice, so too did private enforcement actions. Individuals who felt that they were victims of fraud or misrepresentation in an ICO or STO, for example, started bringing private actions. Government agencies such as the SEC, DOJ, and IRS have also wasted no time investigating and prosecuting individuals and entities for alleged violations of the federal securities laws and tax laws. The increased use of cryptocurrencies has heightened the aggressiveness of certain investigative strategies. The novelty of cryptocurrencies and blockchain technology means it is too soon to tell what will become of this industry. While the technology has clear relevance today, a definitive prediction cannot be made about its future. Whether it flourishes or fails will be revealed only in time.

The final part of this book analyzed how, when, and how deeply blockchain may impact the practice of law and the future of the legal profession for practicing lawyers. It examined the historical relationship between the legal profession and technology and discussed how particular areas of the profession, such as intellectual property, real estate, and criminal defense, may be affected by developing blockchain technology. It also considered some of the practical ways this new technology may affect law firms, such as using blockchain-based record keeping or through a client's desire to pay for legal services with cryptocurrency.

> "This book is titled the "Law of Tomorrow" but tomorrow is happening now. This book outlines what attorneys need to know regarding the future of virtual currencies and its applicability to government regulation efforts and enforcement of laws." Gary Loeffert, retired FBI Special Agent in Charge and Chief of Staff at FBI Headquarters.

This book guides other lawyers and helps them follow in our footsteps. There is a wealth of opportunity in the blockchain space for savvy lawyers who are willing to invest the time into their own education on the subject. With the explosion of activity in both cryptocurrency and blockchain-based businesses, the demand for lawyers that understand the capabilities and limitations of these technologies far outstrips the supply. We are immensely excited about the future of the legal profession and the ways that blockchain and other advancements can help us better serve our clients. We hope that this book has given you some insight into the nature of these technologies and that after reading it, you too now share our excitement for the future of the legal profession.

GLOSSARY

1. **Bitcoin**

Bitcoin was the first and most popular cryptocurrency developed from a white paper in 2008 by developer or group of developers, Satoshi Nakamoto. It is not supervised or controlled by any centralized governmental agency or third party. It is a decentralized currency—meaning that everyone can participate. Bitcoin uses peer-to-peer technology in a secure environment to process and complete transactions.

2. **Block**

A block consists of a transaction or group of transactions that is transferred to the blockchain. Each block contains specific transaction data.

3. **Blockchain**

The blockchain is the distributed, decentralized ledger that securely stores the record of cryptocurrency transactions. These transactions—individually created in blocks—are linked in a peer-to-peer network to form the blockchain. The blockchain is immutable because no one can alter or modify it, and it is transparent because all users can access it and view its history. The first blockchain was the Bitcoin Blockchain. A blockchain can be permissioned, meaning that it exists on a private network of computers and is only accessible to those with access to it. Or a blockchain can be permissionless—meaning that it exists on a network of computers accessible to everyone.

4. **Centralization**

Centralization refers to a system where all transactions are kept on a single server at a single location. A single centralized authority is responsible for all decision-making and control over an activity, company, or process. Traditional financial systems use centralized systems to process, record, and store all transactions.

5. **Cryptocurrency**

Cryptocurrencies are digital forms of money that rely on encryption and consensus algorithms to regulate their trades, transfers, and exchanges. They are decentralized and operate without central authorities. The most common cryptocurrency is Bitcoin. Cryptocurrencies other than Bitcoin—called Altcoins—include Ethereum, Litecoin, Ripple, and Dogecoin.

6. **Cryptography**

Cryptography uses problem-solving techniques and equations to encrypt and decrypt messages. It establishes proof of ownership with cryptocurrencies. This makes it impossible for a user to transfer Bitcoin from an account without having the private key to it. Cryptography uses secure communications that permit only the sender and recipient to view the message.

7. **Decentralization**

Decentralized systems operate without a centralized authority. They do not feature a single authority or a single point that makes decisions. Every computer node on the network makes its own decision, and there is no actor, group, or entity that can control the system without consent of the rest of the parties. A Decentralized Autonomous Organization (DAO) is a company or group of companies that operate based on smart contracts' predefined rules and are stored on the blockchain.

8. **Digital Signature**

The digital signature is a way to verify documents or messages. The digital signature proves that the document or message is authentic because it is from a known sender, and nothing modified or altered it in transit to the recipient.

9. **Distributed-Ledger Technology**

Distributed-ledger technology (DLT) is a system of recording asset transactions and details in multiple copies simultaneously without using centralized systems, storage, or administration. DLT refers to the infrastructure that provides for these transaction processes across a system of networks called nodes. Blockchain is a type of DTL. Thus, all blockchains are DLTs but not all DLTs are blockchains.

10. **Ethereum**

Ethereum is a decentralized blockchain. Ethereum facilitated the first smart-contract platform. Programmer Vitalik Buterin developed Ethereum in 2013. Ether (ETH) is the name given to the Ethereum blockchain network. Ether comes second after Bitcoin in terms of market capitalization.

11. **Fiat Currency**

Fiat currencies are currencies nationally adopted and declared valid by the government. Individuals and companies can use fiat currencies to satisfy various financial obligations because fiat currencies are a legally acceptable form of money. Examples of fiat currencies are the U.S. dollar or the Euro.

12. **Forks**

Forks refer to a network created using a consensus or a protocol as a previous network. These new forks contain either the original network's quality or form a new one. There are hard and soft forks. A hard fork conflicts with the original network and changes the transaction consensus algorithms and data structures. Bitcoin Cash is an example of a hard fork. A soft fork is compatible with the original network. Blocks on the original chain are still compatible on the forked chain, but blocks on the forked chain are not necessarily compatible with blocks on the original chain.

***13. Howey* Test**

The *Howey* Test refers to a U.S. Supreme Court opinion that determined whether an investment contract is a security under the federal securities laws and thus subject to the registration provisions and ongoing disclosure and reporting obligations. The *Howey* Test contains four elements, all of which must be satisfied: (1) an investment of money, (2) in a common enterprise, (3) with a reasonable expectation of profits, and (4) to stem from the efforts of others. *SEC v. W. J. Howey Co.*, 328 U.S. 293 (1946).

14. **ICOs**

An ICO is the first issuance of a coin or token. It is like a public offering of stock, or an IPO. The main difference is that ICOs use blockchain technology. ICOs is a way for businesses to generate capital faster and with less costs than IPOs. The SEC is suspicious of ICOs that fail to register or meet an exemption because ICOs contain various similarities to a security.

15. **Mining**

Mining is verifying and validating transactions and transferring them to the blockchain for a permanent record. Miners works with powerful computers 24/7 that devour energy. To validate a transaction, miners need to work to find the digital key to each block, or the "hash." This step is necessary to validate the transaction and link it to the prior transaction or block, thus allowing for the blockchain to add blocks. To find the key, the miners need to solve a complicated math equation. The first miner or mining pool to successfully solve the equation—or mine the coin—receives a payment reward in the form of a new cryptocurrency.

16. **Node**

The nodes are the computers in the network that form the blockchain network. The nodes process, distribute, and store transaction data. The nodes connect to one another and exchange blockchain data with each other, so the nodes are up to date on the data. As soon as a new block adds to the blockchain, the nodes add copies of the transaction to the network. Miners are a type of node.

17. **Non-Fungible Token (NFT)**

A non-fungible token is a unique token that individuals cannot exchange or substitute with another token. NFTs can represent anything of value such as unique goods, real estate, or artwork. It can also contain anything digital such as GIFs, video games, drawings, and pictures. When someone buys an NFT, they receive ownership to it as their property. The public blockchain records their ownership details, which serves as ownership proof.

18. **Online Cryptocurrency Exchange**

Online cryptocurrency exchanges provide a platform for the trading of cryptocurrencies. Some online exchanges only facilitate crypto purchases and sales, while others also include token exchanges and fiat trading. Cryptocurrency exchanges allow individuals to convert their cryptocurrencies into fiat currencies and then transfer the fiat currency into their bank accounts. The United States as well as the European Union and eastern Asia regulate these exchanges.

19. **Peer-to-Peer Network (P2P)**

Peer-to-peer networks provide a direct connection between participants on a network without using third-party intermediaries. Each computer functions as a server for others and can share files with everyone on the network without these third parties. Users on P2P networks can connect with all other peers also using the network and can transfer value or engage in other transactions.

20. **Proof of Work (PoW)**

One of the two main consensus mechanisms for verifying transactions. With PoW consensus, miners apply both transaction data and a random string of digits to a hashing mathematical formula until the correct solution is found. Once the solution is found, the winning miner shares it with the other miners who verify the proof of work by using the same formula to see if they reach the same result. Once the miners verify the results and the results are the same, the block adds to the blockchain.

The first miner or pool of miners to solve the equation will receive a reward in the form of a new cryptocurrency. PoW consensus demands a lot of energy, or computing power, for verifying transactions. Bitcoin and Ethereum are examples of cryptocurrencies that use PoW.

21. **Proof of Stake (PoS)**

One of the two main consensus mechanisms for verifying transactions. PoS allows miners and other individuals to "stake" or hand over some of their cryptocurrency in exchange for the chance to validate blocks. Validators are selected based on the number of coins they hold. Mining hinges on the proportion of the miner's holdings in the cryptocurrency. The stake—or number of cryptocurrencies handed over—is locked, meaning that users cannot trade or sell or otherwise dispose of the staked cryptocurrency. Miners or individuals who contravene the rules may have their staked cryptocurrencies burned—or destroyed. PoS consensus does not require the same degree of computing power compared to PoW consensus. Cardano and Ethereum 2.0 are examples of cryptocurrencies that use PoS.

22. **Satoshi Nakamoto**

Satoshi Nakamoto was the name used by the developer or group of developers of Bitcoin. Nakamoto authored the seminal white paper in 2008, "Bitcoin: A Peer-to-Peer Electronic Cash System," where he described a fund-transfer system without third-party intermediaries. Nakamoto designed the first blockchain database as a part of writing this white paper and developing Bitcoin.

23. **Security Token**

Security tokens represent a share or interest in a company. These tokens may grant investors certain rights, such as voting rights. The value of security tokens correlates with the value of the company. Security tokens launch with an STO—which are token offerings classified as securities and registered with the SEC but only sold to accredited investors.

24. **Smart Contracts**

A set of rules in computer code stored on the blockchain that automatically executes the terms of the contract upon the occurrence or nonoccurrence of a predefined condition—the triggering event. Smart contracts exist across distributed decentralized networks and operate on blockchain technology. Their operation eliminates using third parties or other intermediaries when processing transactions.

25. **Stablecoin**

Stablecoins are cryptocurrencies that derive their value from some underlying external asset or group of assets (for example, fiat currencies, commodities). They minimize volatility and provide stability because they are pegged to an external asset. Stablecoins are different from other cryptocurrencies such as Bitcoin because Bitcoin's value correlates with how much is mined by computer networks.

26. **Token**

A token refers to programmable or digitalized asset that resides on the blockchain. Individuals and companies can use tokens for various purposes including making purchases, serving some utility, and investment.

27. **Tokenization**

Tokenization is turning sensitive information into a random digital equivalent, or token, that represents the original value. Tokenization converts assets into tokens and then records and stores those tokens on the blockchain. As applied to real estate, tokenization is representing ownership or ownership interests of a type of real estate with tokens.

28. **Utility Token**

Individuals and companies issue utility tokens only to fund the development of a project or a cryptocurrency. They are issued to a closed ecosystem of individuals, such as employees of the company issuing the utility token. The value of these tokens is unrelated to the value of the company. Utility tokens are not investment contracts or securities; therefore, individuals do not have to register them.

29. **Wallet**

A wallet is a digital storage file that holds an individual's coins and tokens. Each wallet has an address that others use to send funds. An individual can have either a cold wallet or a hot wallet. A cold wallet is stored on a platform disconnected from the internet. Because they are not connected to the internet, cold wallets protect against cyber threats and other vulnerabilities. A hot wallet connects to the internet. It is faster and easier to trade cryptocurrencies with a hot wallet, but also more susceptible to online threats and cyber-attacks.

30. **51% Attack**

A 51% attack occurs when more than half of the computing power—more than half of the miners—launch an attack on the nodes. If that miner controls at least 51% of the network, he can change the network, steal assets, engage in double spending of the same coins, or stop transaction confirmations.

Made in United States
North Haven, CT
10 November 2026

22096036R00095